CRIME, G
Why I Left th

MW01278022

....

CHRIS BANSON as told to MARY MOSS

COPYRIGHT © Mary Moss 2016
All rights reserved

DEDICATION
In Memoriam to my friend Ed
Rest in peace, good buddy

Acknowledgments

Many thanks and much appreciation to FRANCISCO MORALES for his great cover design. I've never dreamed that an artist could immediately "intuit" what I had in mind for the artwork. I wish you much success in your career as an artist.

A big backpat of thanks and gratitude to friends Ken J. and Dave T., whose weary eyes read and reread every draft and gave me very valuable feedback (and caught typos). Thanks, guys. Dinner's on me next time.

Appreciation goes to Georgia Durante, whose own book first inspired me to tell my story. Your personal encouragement motivated me to get this book out there for the world to read. I won't forget your kindness.

* * * * *

AUTHOR'S NOTE

Going back to try to recall all those years in the past was an absorbing task. My effort was made easier by Ms. Moss, who assisted me with staying on subject and moving the story along. While I have used some original names in this memoir, there were a few that necessarily had to be changed. Which, come to think of it, isn't really unusual when you consider the subject . . .

CRIME, GREED & LIES
Why I Left the Rochester Mob

PROLOGUE

Few individuals who performed in my role for the Mob have survived to tell about it. Even fewer are allowed to walk away from the organization in good standing and with no strings attached. I've been extremely lucky; after forty-some years, I finally feel easier in my mind, enough to stop looking over my shoulder constantly and sitting with my back to the wall in restaurants and other public places. Ask my wife, though, and she'll tell you that I really still prefer to sit facing the door. That's because I sure haven't forgotten what those days were like and what I did during my days working in organized crime.

For historical context, since I'm not Italian descent, I couldn't be genuinely called a *soldier*, even thought I performed the duties of one. Rather, I would have been classified by the Mob as an *associate*. As such, I served as a bodyguard and chauffer for several Mob bosses. Sometimes my passengers included one of the Valenti brothers (Stan and Frank) or some other notorious *Mafia* figure.

The daily danger that came with the job meant constantly looking over my shoulder, and carrying at least one—sometimes two—loaded weapons. So, I wasn't just a driver--I was actually scrving as a soldicr, right whcrc thc action was, participating fully. The bodyguarding role kept my adrenaline running high. Crouching down behind garbage dumpsters with bullets zinging past or ricocheting off the metal made it flow all the more. There's nothing like living on the edge, they say. And, I guess it's true, too, that what doesn't kill you makes ya stronger!

Because of my loyalty, high energy, and fearless "can do" attitude within the organization, my little family and I were able to live at a much higher standard than my regular day job could possibly afford. That's where greed really rears its ugly head: snowmobiles, ponies, good clothes, and new cars became the norm. My wife could buy a dress without considering the price first.

The downside is that, eventually, someone has to pay a price for this standard of living. And, it sure wasn't the Mob—hell, they had so much money, it was flying around like a whirlwind of autumn leaves. They didn't have to worry about "going over budget." More dough kept rolling in all the time.

Instead of the organization suffering the consequences, *I* was the one who wound up paying, over a few years, for this high-on-the-hog lifestyle. From the fateful day I took the Mafia loyalty oath to the end of about three years, my marriage spiraled downward and ended in an irretrievable shambles. I was drinking too much and not spending enough time at home. My children were being neglected and unsupervised. And I hated myself for what I'd done just for the thrill and glory--those adrenaline rushes and nonstop sex--and, of course, the good ol' Dollar Green.

When I set out to write this book, I intended to leave out the personal stuff and focus exclusively on my days with the Rochester Mafia in terms of "business"--criminal activity. The power and machinations of organized crime have fascinated many people over the decades, and are still drawing in fans and readers. It was constant crime, greed, and lies--every day.

But as I continued to recall and articulate the details of those days for this book, I finally had to admit that much of my life back then also revolved around sex. Sex with my wife, sex with other women, seeing my wife have sex with Mob associates, sex within the Mob activities--it was all tangled up together. Talking about how that affected my family life means getting up close and personal in ways you may find objectionable.

So, reader be warned—there's a lot more sex in this book than you'll find in most true stories from the world of the *Mafia*. While Georgia Durante's story of her days with them, "The Company She Keeps," basically centers around lots of romance and interpersonal intrigue, it doesn't tell it the way I'm going to. That means this book really isn't intended for young, impressionable teenage boys, although it may find its way into their hands. Don't say I didn't warn you!

There's one phrase that has continually come to mind as I've gone over this very dynamic part of my life: *What was I thinking?* Why did I think I was invincible and so special that joining the Mob wouldn't turn my life upside down? And, what man in his right mind would be so naive as to deliberately lead his young, inexperienced wife into the sexy 60's pastime of "swinging" and strip poker--and then not understand why she didn't stay faithful?

Not engaging in serious, critical thinking was what got me in over my head, in so many ways. I never took the time to calm down and truly explore my options before acting. In short, I wasn't one to weigh the alternatives before mindlessly jumping into the deep end of the pool.

Even after my first marriage crashed with a loud "boom," I still didn't stand back and take some time to get my bearings. Instead, I jumped headfirst into another relationship so as to "get even" with my philandering ex-wife. (But that's another story for a future book.) So, now, in my mid 70's, I still wonder, what I was thinking?

Well, it was what it was. As the saying goes, "get in, sit down, shut up, and hang on" as we go for a ride like no other and you experience the life of a Mob team member through this memoir.

CHAPTER ONE

The winter snow had finally melted away and the sun was shining warmly, but my blood was running cold. I was sitting in a cramped, messy office at the famous Rochester, NY Farmer's Market, with the cold, hard steel of a .45 semi-automatic pistol pressed to my temple. The harsh voice of *Alphonse* (A.J.) Camp hit my ears with a terrifying message.

"We are a family, and we take care of our own. But, if you fuck with us, you're dead."

A lot of thoughts flashed through my mind. Who were these guys, really? I'd heard rumors that the *Mafia*, or "Mob," was active in Rochester, and even some mention about vendors at the Farmer's Market being involved in organized crime. But, up to then, I'd never encountered any solid evidence or seen direct proof that this was so. Most of what I knew was gleaned from a few clips from gangster movies about Al Capone and his buddies.

Immediately, I had a lot of questions begging for answers. Would these men really shoot me, no questions asked? Obviously, everything hinged on a "Yes" or "No" answer from me right now. Was I going to accept the offer being made, or was good sense going to prevail and spur me to run for my life, metaphorically if not literally speaking?

Readers might wonder how the heck I had wound up there, in the company of the *Mafia* at the Market, in the first place. That's a story in itself, and I'll discuss it as I go along.

But, back to that crucial moment. As my brief reverie ended, I was still there with A.J. standing beside me, pressing that .45 against my temple and speaking those unforgettable words. I was being offered a job with the *Mafia* and had to make a decision.

Then, Joe Camp spoke. "Chris, do you understand? Do you want to work with us?"

I had to say something. Finally, I broke my silence; I nodded my head and croaked, "Understood. Yes."

Apparently satisfied that I'd gotten the message and would comply, A.J. put the .45 away and sat down. Joe smiled reassuringly. Boy, was I relieved to know that gun was out of sight!

"I'm sure you'll do just fine, Chris." Joe spoke in a friendly voice. "And, we can help you get new clients for your produce company, too. Does that sound like something you'd like to do?"

I still had no idea of what I was getting myself into, but the desire to make more money was always there. Greed is a good master. And, frankly, the prospect was exciting; I was a bit of a "drama queen" anyway, and thrived on adrenaline rushes. So, I nodded again and said that their ideas all sounded good.

All the while, a cold trickle of fear was still running—no, galloping--through my body, and, at the same time, it was so thrilling! I had been raised not to fear anything or anybody. What A.J. and Joe had said, along with that gun, sure got my attention, it sounded good, and now the next move was up to me.

I agreed to their terms and was then warmly received into The Family. This was all living proof that what I'd taken as rumors about the *Mafia* being involved at the Market was, in fact, the gospel truth. Joe and A.J. took me through the *Omerta* loyalty oath, the traditional Mafia kiss, and the usual rituals that all new "family members" experience. This was all done in the presence of a committee of six or seven other people. I had to swear to protect them and their code of honor, but due to my lack of Italian heritage, I didn't take the usual Mafia *soldier's* oath.

For those who don't know, *Omerta* is a code of honor that places importance on silence, non-cooperation with authorities, and non-interference in the illegal actions of others. According to references, *Omerta* originated and remains common in the regions of Corsica, Sardinia, and Southern Italy. That's where the Sicilian *Mafia* and *Mafia*-type criminal organizations are strong. The code also exists--to a lesser extent--in certain neighborhoods where the Italian-American *Mafia* has influence, as it did then in Rochester as well as other enclaves here in North America and countries such as Germany, Canada, and Australia.

Retaliation against informers is common in criminal circles, where informers are known as "rats" or "snitches," just as they are today in the street gangs and crime-ridden neighborhoods here in America.

The fact that I wouldn't ever be accorded the official designation of Mob *soldier* didn't matter to me. My gawd, I realized, I'm about to become a gangster! What would Grandpa think, or my dad? It wasn't right, I knew, yet I couldn't resist the temptation, the prospective thrill, and the enticements of money and power.

"Now, we'll talk again in a few days," Joe stated. "One more thing--will your wife be okay with you working more hours, maybe at night?"

If she wasn't now, she would be, I figured. Our little family needed more money--that was for sure. It was arranged that Joe and I would meet again a few days later, in the office.

CHAPTER TWO

My sales job in the produce industry connected me back to my early childhood days, which I spent watching and helping my grandpa grow and sell fresh produce in Watertown. He used his old farm truck as an open farmer's market of sorts, and had many steady customers every week. They'd queue up to buy baskets of tomatoes, pounds of onions, sacks of potatoes, and whatever else Grandpa was selling that day. I learned how to please the customer, make change, and smile a lot.

I didn't start out living on that farm, but wound up there when I was close to four years old. My father had been overseas in the Army during the early forties, and while he was gone his wife, my mother, apparently couldn't stand being alone. My older brother was eight, our sister was not quite six, and I was just about three.

One day, our mother dropped us off at another family's home (I'll call them Mr. and Mrs. Brown) and then simply disappeared from our lives. My memories of that time are a bit fuzzy because I was so young, but even then I could see that the lady of the house clearly didn't want us there. Her husband treated us more kindly--we were akin to foster children then, without a government subsidy--but I hated living there.

It was with great relief when, many months later, our father hastened up the sidewalk to the front door. I'll never forget the sight of him, carrying his military cap. We three children were overjoyed as Dad explained to the Browns that he'd been searching for us for several weeks. He'd been discharged from the military and came back to what had been his home with us, but everyone was gone. His wife was nowhere to be found. He was very worried about what had happened to us, his children. After making tireless inquiries and driving all over the county, he finally found out where we were, and hurried to get us.

Obviously, we all needed a home, including Dad, and so that's how we wound up going to live on his parents' farm for a while. Ironically, the Browns' home was less than 10 miles away from the farm. We had been so close to our kin when our Mother left, but we didn't know it at the time. I still can't figure out why, if she just didn't want us anymore, she didn't simply take us to grandpa's farm right away.

I loved my grandparents and they loved me and my brother and sister. They were both committed to hard work and doing what needed to be done. Resourceful and energetic, they made sure we all had plenty to eat and a chance to live a reasonably happy life.

My farm duties started out with simple things, like going out to the chicken house and gathering eggs. I grew physically strong and learned my way around farm animals as well as tractors, selling produce, and doing my share of hard work as I grew.

Grandpa kept the aforementioned chickens, grew vegetables, and generally made a living for all of us by selling eggs and garden produce in a nearby large town. His big workhorses pulled various plows and other farm implements needed to till the ground for the crops. My daily joy came in a large dose when I was allowed to help Grandpa in the barn. Aside from a small percentage of kids who find horses frightening, most youngsters love horses and being around them. I was no exception. Feeding those big horses was such a thrill; they were gentle but so alive! Carefully, I brushed and curried them as high up as I could reach, and then used a milking stool to reach their backs. I loved their earthy smell, gentle snorting noises, and the way they'd whinny when they saw me coming with treats, such as fresh carrots. I'd already filled their mangers with fresh hay, and they easily tolerated the grooming while they munched their food. Occasionally, I would bring their feedbags with generous helpings of oats, and Grandpa would let me help him slide them over the horses' heads. He even let me brush out their fetlocks, which collected mud constantly.

Grandma would scold, "Now, John, you mustn't let Chris get around those horses' feet! Why, they could step right on him!"

In reply, Grandpa would brush off her warnings as one might ward off a pesky fly or something.

"Minnie, he'll be just fine. He knows what to do and so do the horses."

And, he was right.

As time went on, I was allowed to actually "drive" those horses when we hauled wagonloads of hay from the field back to the barn. After that, I graduated to being allowed to hold the reins when we traversed the back-country roads during various outings.

I was pretty small for my age, but it wasn't long before I mastered the art of climbing up on a fence or stump to mount one of those horses and go for a ride. Naturally, I just *had* to learn to be a stunt man, running and jumping up from the ground onto their backs, like the Lone Ranger or something. Only, there wasn't usually a saddle to catch my butt, just the bare back of the animal. Those big horses were patient and very tolerant of my leaps onto their backs, and I thought I was doing an amazing thing. Grandpa just shook his head and smiled. It was nothing he hadn't already done himself as a youngster. But he admitted, "You do have a way with those horses, son."

By then, I'd learned the thrill that comes from holding the reins and learning to signal the horses to turn, go, and stop. The surging power of their muscles—all that horsepower—came right up through the reins to my hands. It was like electricity, and I respected how much those horses responded and moved or stopped. The animals were gentle and didn't go for speed when I rode them, but it was fun just the same.

Those days on the farm were pleasant, and they flew by. Dad married again; his new wife, Gertie, was a widow with two young sons. In a short time, Gertie and Dad had produced two more children, a girl and a boy. We had moved to our own home near town but still spent lots of time with our grandparents.

However, we were on our own as a family and didn't have a farm like the grandparents on which to grow our food. A household of seven kids and two adults equated to way too many mouths to feed. Gertie and Dad both worked full-time. She drove around most of the night, picking up and delivering newspapers all the way from Watertown to where we lived. When she returned home, she'd hand the car keys to Dad and he'd head out to his job.

But, there simply wasn't enough money coming in. So, my brother went to live and work on a nearby farm, and by age 11, I, too, was capable of earning a living. So, one day, I left home to work for room and board and $1.00 a day on a nearby farm run by a kind man named Vern Hopkins. I didn't just run off and do that; I'd previously met Mr. Hopkins in Watertown while helping Grandpa with the produce truck, and he offered me the job. My dad knew there wasn't much choice, so he agreed.

From Day One, I'd been brought up to be frugal, and I tucked away those hard-earned dollars. When Mr. Hopkins saw my determination to hang on to my money, he took me to the local bank and helped me open my own checking account. I deposited my hard-earned cash there, every week. Sometimes I could make a little extra doing odd jobs on other farms and I'd save that extra money, too. Then, each Sunday, when my Dad came to pick me up to spend the day with the family, I would proudly give him $5 of the $7+ I'd earned that week.

One day, I found out that Dad was going to need a new pair of eyeglasses that would cost $70. So, I saved up my money and was soon able to give him $60 to help pay for them. Was he ever surprised--and grateful--when I handed him an actual check I'd written out for the amount. He stared at me and then I saw tears in his eyes.

"Thank you, Son," he managed to say. I think he was quite surprised.

I may have been a good farmhand and money manager, but neighbors of Vern Hopkins used to razz him about having hired a diminutive little pipsqueak like me.

"Why, that young'un ain't big enough to pick a pail of peas, Vern," they'd say.

Vern would squint his eyes at these naysayers, and reply something to the effect, "Say all you want about his size. I say that dynamite comes in small packages. This little guy is a hard worker and as strong as an ox."

His eyes would twinkle and he'd chuckle to himself.

He wasn't wrong. I quickly grew strong, developing my muscles as I bucked bales of hay and lifted milk cans and other heavy things. Most boys aren't as strong at age 11, I know that. I was learning to do a man's work and building the muscle necessary to do it.

All of that hard work and responsibility meant I had to grow up fast. Of course, when you leave home and start working for a living at such a young age, get seduced by an adult woman at age 12 (and, coincidentally, learn to drive her husband's car during that same period), you're already in the fast lane, focusing on typically adult fun, right? Speaking of which, there was another important set of muscles in my body that were about ready for exercise. I was starting to become aware of that.

My early seduction took place one day back when I was working on that farm. I spent my days tending to the milking chores first, including mucking out the barn stalls, etc. Neighbors weren't exactly right next door, but we weren't completely isolated, either; there were adjacent farms and a small town was about a thirty-minute walk from the farmhouse. When I finished my chores for the day, I was free to go find my own fun--on foot, of course. While I liked being around Mr. and Mrs. Hopkins, I also wanted to be around kids my age. I only got to see my brother and sister on Sunday, and didn't always get to school. So, I did my socializing where I could.

One day, I was over at a neighboring farm where a girl named Janie lived. We were both about the same age and in the same class at the local school (which, as I said, I attended only sporadically). Like most country kids, we came into puberty at ages younger than some of our peers. Anyway, we were fooling around outside her house, and I was playing with her tits. Janie was well-developed for her age. Suddenly, a woman who lived across the road happened to come out into her front yard, saw us, and came over in a hurry.

"You stop that right now!" she exclaimed, and led me away, after telling Janie to go into the house. I thought she was just going to send me home, too, but instead, she looked at me closely and said, "If you're going to start playing around with girls, you need to learn to do it right. Come in here with me."

She accompanied me back to her house and opened the front porch door.

Her name was Lottie, and boy, did she show me a lot! I guess she was in her early thirties then; she was dark-haired, petite, and attractive. Lottie was probably in her early 30's then. I knew from neighborhood gossip that her husband was quite a drunk. He'd work nights and then come home loaded and sleep away most of the day in a room upstairs. So, his presence wasn't a problem.

Lottie led me into the downstairs bedroom. Keep in mind that I was not a big, hulking kid. I probably weighed about 110 lbs. soaking wet, but doing farm work had made me physically strong and wiry.

Apparently, Lottie wasn't being "taken care of" by her drunken husband and had figured I'd do all right as a bed partner. She proceeded to show me "where the shit hit the buckwheat." Naturally, I was all eyes as she removed her dress, exposing a very pretty pair of womanly breasts and that fascinating triangle of dark pubic hair down below. I'd never seen such things before so "up close and personal," and it wasn't long before I was undressed, too, and finding out how fun it was to touch and kiss those tits and play with her pussy. Lottie taught me how to touch her body in ways that aroused her. Soon, we were both pretty stimulated and I learned that day what my dick was really meant to do. I was in hog heaven.

For the next few years, (yes, years!), I would nip over to Lottie's whenever time allowed, for my sex education classes. No matter where I lived, I knew I could have sex with her whenever I wanted. Over time, she showed me all the pleasures and intricacies of oral sex, too—both giving and receiving.

"Now, Chris, some ladies like to have this done on them," she would say, and we'd practice some new technique until I had it perfected.

Today, most people would label this whole thing as child sexual abuse. Me? I thought it was finer than frog hair! I was miles ahead of my male peers, who only daydreamed about this stuff. While they were salivating over *Playboy* magazine centerfolds, I had the real thing whenever I wanted, as often as I wanted. I'm sure Vern wondered why I spent so much of my spare time over at Lottie's.

Having been awakened to the pleasures of the flesh at the very young age of 12, and living on a farm away from my family, no one taught me the concept of sublimation or how to keep that monster in my underwear from taking over my life. I only saw my dad on Sundays when he would pick me up at the farm for a day in town with the family, and we never talked about sex. My brother was hardly ever around, either, so I couldn't talk to him. There was no guidance or parenting by anyone, so I had no way of knowing that it wasn't okay or appropriate for a young boy to be sexually active. I'm sure they'd all have been horrified if they'd known what was going on.

Fast forward a couple of years, and I was 14. I'd already learned how to drive the more "modern" horsepower generated by the engine in Grandpa's produce delivery truck. Although I was small and short, I could manage to turn the steering wheel, let out the clutch, give it the gas, and there we went, down the back roads. I was driving for real! When I went home on Sundays, we'd usually stop by the grandparent's farm and that's when I got to drive the truck.

Soon I was truly a young man. Then, my attention focused on just five things: Sex, money, booze, rock and roll—oh, and driving fast cars. You notice I put sex first, of course; when testosterone flows, desire results. Anyway, what more could a randy young guy want? Those five things made the world go around during my younger days.

Being an independent, invincible young fella, my self-confidence was sky-high when I started dating girls my age and I was coercing them into sex on the first or second date. By the time I was 16, I'd been driving cars for years, had one available for these "dates," and was known for being what most people call a "bad boy." The point is, I was already miles ahead of my male chums who could only dream of getting pussy on a regular basis, let alone being experienced in driving a car.

 Of course, those North Country girls were a pretty horny bunch, themselves; my sexual overtures weren't rejected very often. And, since I could always find sex somewhere, including with Lottie, I never forced or insisted. "No" meant "No" to me, and I respected the girl's choice and right to say it.

Horsepower and testosterone took over and more or less ran my life for a while. It was quite a combination. I became quite skillful at driving cars and it wasn't long before I was offered to substitute for a driver at the local stock car races. Although I was officially underage, my driving abilities clouded the judgment of the people at the track. It was tons of fun and these experiences continued to fuel my love of driving at high speeds.

The fact is, I was well-known in the Watertown area for being able to outrun the cops--always. During those years, I *never* got pulled over or received a speeding ticket, due to the simple fact that law enforcement didn't have drivers as good as me. The police would chase me, sure, but I had a hat bag of tricks to outsmart them every time. One local officer habitually set out to get me and I'd leave him sitting in the dust, shaking his fist. Those were fun times and set the scene for my later using fast driving as a moneymaker for myself with the Mob.

Back then, my favorite car for those kinds of chases was a 1949 Ford, although I also liked the big Buicks. Give me a heavy, rear-wheel drive vehicle and I'd board her (press the gas pedal to the floorboard), taking curves and sharp turns like butter at 90-110 mph. Even on two wheels, I could keep control of the car.

One time I rounded a curve at ninety and--oops! There was a farmer's wagon and horses straight ahead on the road. The only thing I could do was wheel the car around them, causing it to spin around in three "doughnuts," and then I gave 'er the gas and we kept going. My younger stepbrother, sitting beside me, was full of admiration and egged me on to do "something else as fun" as that had been. Fortunately, I had to sense to tone things down and drive a little slower, at least, for a couple of hours.

Sadly, my employer, Mr. Hopkins, had suddenly keeled over and died one morning, and his wife bravely thought she could continue running their farm, but it didn't work out. At age 15 I'd gone to work on another dairy farm for Bill Mason. I'd also acquired an old beater Ford, but couldn't afford the license or insurance for it, so it sat there out behind the barn.

By then, though, I needed to be out and about; after all, there were pretty young women out there and stuff going on that made milking cows seem pretty dull. I was always creative and inventive when it came to making my own fun. Give me a problem to solve and I'd usually come up with a solution in short order. So, I developed a technique of waiting at night until the Mason's house was quiet and then I'd go outside, quietly remove the license plates from Bill's car, and attach them to my old Ford. Then I'd set off to go see my girl friend and get rowdy somewhere.

I loved to outdrive the local cops just for fun. I'd see how fast I could take certain curves (preferably in a contest with some other fool). I thought I was something. Hell, I had my hair slicked back in a D.A. like James Dean, with the requisite pack of cigarettes tucked into the sleeve of my white T-shirt. So, I was cooler than cool.

When I was dating a girl named Jody in a nearby small town, her father was the sheriff in a larger town a few miles away. There I was, about 15 years old and driving a car with no license. Also, the car was not street legal, but the girl's father liked me and wanted his daughter to be happy. So, he told me to be especially careful and to only drive at normal speed from the farm to his house.

"Stay off the main roads," he ordered me. "I don't want you to get pulled over by the local guy."

Well, that rule didn't hold water. Of course, I just had to keep going fast and race down the main highway. And, of course, the local cop was always trying to catch me. Sometimes, I'd drive with my headlights off, put the car in neutral gear, and let it coast so he couldn't hear my cut-outs and locate me that way. Then I'd lose him, which really pissed him off.

Finally, he told Jody's father about me, and her loving dad then told the local cop to back off and he'd take care of it.

After being scolded, I behaved like a good little boy for a while and slowed down as I drove past the sheriff. Sometimes, I would do the license plate switch routine, using the plates off Bill's car, and take my girl to the movies over in Watertown. Like I said, I never got stopped by law enforcement during those times.

Yeah, Jody's father was good to me, and so was his daughter, if you know what I mean. Of course, my glorious and much-deserved reputation of being a "fast fellow" with the girls kept things moving along in that department. You get the picture, I'm sure. Keep in mind that this was freestyle/free love sex, totally removed from the higher class (and higher paying) prostitution that I was introduced to later on with the Mob. Back then, I simply knew what a car's backseat was really for and used it accordingly. Those big cars we drove back then were nice and roomy. Sure, I was horny and full of testostcrone, but I was a teenage boy; that's pretty normal.

My boss on the dairy farm frequently objected. "Chris," he'd say, "All this helling around is either gonna kill you or you're gonna knock up some gal and then the frying pan will really be in the fire."

He'd shake his head, smiling, for he had been no angel himself, but was trying his best to be a sort of surrogate father to me since I wasn't around my own dad very often. I had no male family role model to talk to or give me advice. So, I was footloose and fancy free with no mature adult guidance.

Learning what was taught in school didn't interest me much. What little time I spent at the school was flirting--and worse--with the girls every chance I got. One day, Susan Woodson and I were messing around in a quiet hall during lunch time. Things heated up fast and we wound up seeking more privacy in the janitor's closet. She hiked up her skirt and obligingly put one foot on an upended mop bucket, and I was in her, hot and hard. We were enjoying ourselves immensely and then suddenly, the closet door was yanked open. There stood the school librarian, Mrs. Roberts.

That closet was on the wall right across from the library and she must have seen us go in or heard us. At any rate, she raged at us to "stop this instant," and as I tucked things back in and zipped up, I laughed and said, "Ah, hell, you're just jealous that you didn't get done first" or something like that.

Mrs. Roberts turned nineteen shades of purple and her voice went into high soprano. She physically yanked Susan out into the hallway, hissing at her to go to the girls' room and do what needed to be done. Meanwhile, I was sent to the dreaded Principal's office to receive a thorny lecture on my sins and a stern warning that I'd be out on my ear after the next, slightest infraction of school rules and common decency.

Who cares? Who needs a book-learned education? That was my attitude and now I look back at where it got me--nowhere.

By the time I was 17, rock and roll was also a big part of my scene. I frequently entertained my chums (and impressed the girls) at a local soda fountain with a perfect imitation of Elvis Presley's film version of his hit song, "Jailhouse Rock." I was into Elvis and Jerry Lee Lewis big time—they were my role models. Half the time I was pretty tanked up on beer or something stronger, too. It was all part of the fun. It loosened me up and I thought I deserved it as a reward for hard work. I worked on several dairy farms in the area, hefting everything from hay bales to milk cans (and milking cows, too.) Finally, I could afford to pay for the license and car insurance and was openly driving my Ford whenever time allowed.

Along with loving rock and roll, I was big into dancing and went out every weekend with different girls. We'd do the swing, the stroll, the bop, and everything else that was the current rage. Then, on the way home, we'd get our rhythm together in another way. There was one girl I went out with a lot; she had one brown eye and one blue eye. This fascinated me; I thought she was quite unique and I liked that I could claim her as "my girl" as well as being her regular lover. Even though I wasn't faithful to her, she didn't mind being known as my steady. She was a good dancer and liked to sing; sometimes the local bands would let her get up on the bandstand and do a couple of songs. We had a really hot sexual relationship, that's for sure.

Then there was Jeanette, and Karen, and Phyllis, and--way too many to get into here. Telling about all of them would turn this into a porn novel. But there were many. As I look back on my teenage philandering days, I marvel that I never knocked up any of those girls, although I suppose there could be a couple of people around Watertown who have always wondered who the hell their father was . . .

Little did I realize then, that, in a grown man's world, pussy is *always* his desire and goal, and, too often, the quest for it will be his downfall. History has shown this to be an absolute truth. Just look at all of the politicians, media stars, clergy, and other men who've been brought down due to not being able to keep their pants zipped up. What is it the French say—*cherchez la femme*? We never stop looking for or at it when it walks by. I'm 75 and I'm still mightily interested, just ask my wife!

Anyway, since my carnal desires were being satisfied at that time, and I had a car in which to speed and booze to drink, the only thing I lacked in life was plentiful money. I knew that was going to have to change somehow but I didn't have a concrete plan for it just then.

But, the time was coming. That impetuous, crazy teenage lifestyle I'd led took a turn for the more serious by the time I was 18. I was in a small town in upstate New York, on my way home from a medical appointment due to a car accident while riding with a friend and my stepbrother (the accident was his fault). My stepmother, Gertie, was driving and we stopped at the local post office.

I stood by the car while she went in, since standing was actually less painful than sitting. Just then, a pretty girl came out of the building, and I did a double take. She had shoulder-length brown hair and big brown eyes and I was instantly attracted to her. So, I said "Hi" and she did the same. We started talking, and by the time Gertie came back to the car, I'd made a date with that girl. Her name was Norma.

When I got back to the farm that night, I dramatically announced to my employer that I'd met my future wife. He just shook his head, knowing that for the past several months, I'd been going with a girl from Canada named Marcie. I'd spent every weekend up there, mostly having sex with her.

What was crazy about that relationship was that her parents seemed to think I was just perfect for their daughter, and they made it easy for us to sleep together, fuck all night, and then go downstairs for breakfast with their full approval. They were very warm and friendly, treating me just as though I was part of the family. I'd actually been contemplating the idea of marriage with Marcie when I met Norma. Suddenly, Canada seemed too far to go and I was totally preoccupied with my new flame.

Norma and I dated for several weeks before getting sexually involved. That was new behavior for me. I was head over heels in love, completely infatuated, bamboozled, and enthralled with the girl. She was just 17 and I was a year older. I worshipped and respected her to the Nth degree and I didn't want to rush things. For once, I took my time in working up to having sex with a girl. She was different and I treated the whole relationship with awe and wonder; I believed I'd finally found true, everlasting love and that there'd never be anyone else for either of us.

One night, Norma and I had been making out for hours. The car windows were steamed up and so were we. I'd been fingering her pussy and working her up until she was on fire. I didn't want to wait any longer, and finally, neither did she. Norma lost her virginity in that back seat with great enthusiasm, having orgasm after orgasm. I think my back still has scars from her nails digging into me as she went crazy. She just couldn't get enough.

From then on, we were completely inseparable and fucking whenever opportunity allowed. But we did at least make a pretense of "going out" for normal dates that involved riding around, stopping for a Coke, etc. Sometimes we double-dated with friends, going to drive-ins and dances.

One time, she was in the car with me on our way out for the evening, and I'd agreed to race a guy for money; his car was new. He thought he was a hotshot driver and could best me. Well, I went one up on him; I'd borrowed a friend's Buick and knew what it could do. I took turns and curves, passing the other guy with that Buick up on two wheels as I beat him to a prearranged spot. Norma hung onto my leg and she dug her nails right through the denim of my work pants. God, she actually drew blood, she dug in so hard!

When we reached the finish line, so to speak, several friends were standing around to witness the event. They saw the blood on my pants, thought it was from Norma, and started razzing me about how it must have really been a good run. I didn't care; I'd won both the race and the lady. They didn't know that I'd already deflowered her several weeks earlier.

Norma was very impressed by my fearlessness and professional driving abilities. One night, I'd had too much to drink (who, me??) and Norma had to drive me home. I lay in the back seat. On the way home, she was pulled over by a local cop, and he didn't see me there in the back seat. Well, the son-of-a-bitch tried to put the make on Norma, and then I suddenly jumped up and was in his face. He was shocked and tried to make excuses, but there was no getting around what he'd done. We had him by the balls and he knew it. A cop who tried to sexually coerce a teenage girl wasn't okay; all she had to do was go back home and tell her family, and that cop would lose his job or worse. From that night on, I could do as I damned well pleased and he would not chase after me. Boy, did I take advantage of that situation!

On a pleasant summer evening, Norma and I were driving around. We had all of the windows down and the radio was on, of course. Naturally, I was keeping my speed in time with the fast music that played. We were on a main road, and suddenly we met a sheriff's deputy coming toward us. My speedometer was hovering at the 75-mph mark. When the deputy went past us, I saw his brake lights flash on. Uh-oh.

I told Norma to hang on, and I continued down the road a little way and then slammed on *my* brakes. I spun that big car around and headed back the other way. Here came the deputy, lights and siren on, coming right at us--and right past us, of course, going in the opposite direction.

But once again, the damned fool hit his brakes. Apparently, he was determined to pull me over and wasn't giving up. I knew he would turn around and come after me, soI kept going for a short distance, then repeated my earlier action of braking to a stop and spinning the car around to face the opposite direction. Instantly, I boarded the accelerator and we head back at high speed. Once again, here came the deputy like a bat out of hell, lights and siren on full bore. And, once again, I pressed the gas pedal to the floor and we roared past him going the other way. He knew he was beaten and just threw his hands up in the air in surrender and kept going. It was hysterically funny to see, just like something out of a cops-and-robbers movie or something.

Finally, I slowed down a little, turned onto a back road, and stayed off main roads for a while. We didn't see the deputy again that night. But Norma and I were convulsed in laughter when we parked later.

"Did you see--see--the look on his face?" She spluttered. "It was so funny!"

I agreed. It's remained one of my favorite memories about my teenage driving days.

Naturally, my carefree fun and luck couldn't go on forever. I was driving like a bat out of hell all the time and also fucking my brains out with my girl. Dumb ass me, never one to use condoms (who wants to take a bath with their socks on? I used to say), it wasn't long before I'd knocked up that Girl of My Dreams. I already knew she was The One, so, romantic dumb shit that I was, when she told me she was pregnant, I didn't give it a second thought. I immediately proposed marriage and she accepted.

It was the late 1950's then. We lived in a small town where unwed motherhood was still severely frowned upon by the older generation. I didn't really care too much about that; I was very willing to marry Norma and settle down. Secretly, I did think it was all very romantic, and I could hardly wait to be a father. I'd bought into the little-house-with-the-white-picket-fence vision, just like so many young American dreamers back in the late 1950's. I was through sowing my wild oats and wanted to settle down. My girl was beautiful, sexy, and everything I'd ever wanted. I couldn't imagine life without her and I put her up on a very tall pedestal; she could do no wrong and I was deeply in love. Norma and I would have our little family and live happily ever after. Life would finally be like it should have been when I was a child, with a yard full of giggling children playing hide-and-go-seek and tag. I could see us in a few years, sitting on a backyard patio and watching our children while we smiled and sipped iced tea. Of course, that ridiculous dream bubble would burst before long, but it was fun while it lasted.

As we all know, with parenthood and marriage come responsibilities and many expenses. My wife and first child, a baby girl, and I moved from the North Country of upstate New York down to a small community on the outskirts of Rochester. We were still in upstate New York, but in a much different world. Constant change was certainly the watchword, but more changes were about to happen than I ever could have foreseen in my freewheeling, hell-seeking days.

After my family and I had moved near the city, I sought employment in the area. It wasn't long before I was hired by a large, commercial produce vendor. The company supplied area restaurants and grocery stores. Having worked in grandpa's big truck garden and helped him sell produce off his truck, it was a good use of my experience and knowledge.

As my delivery and sales routine became established, I naturally got acquainted with the various Market vendors, which included the *Campanellas* (known locally just as The Camps), the *Valenti* brothers, Joe the Banana Man, and others. That's what initially put me into proximity with the Mob guys. But, I didn't know about their secrets at the time; they were just folks I bought produce from every week.

As it happened, my lovely wife was already pregnant again with our third child, so another mouth to feed was in the offing. Yes, you did the math right; there's just one year difference in age between our first and second children, and less than two years later the third child came along. And, that was how I came to be at the Rochester Farmer's Market, being propositioned by the *Mafia*. I needed to make more money and the Mob needed me to do help them do their dirty work. It was a win-win situation, or so I thought. Easy money was too tempting to resist. I'd been struggling and working my ass off ever since I was 11 years old and now I was really boxed into a corner. Do I turn down what could be the offer of my life, or do I make a move towards living the high roller style? I did have to make a decision.

In retrospect, I realized that word about my ambitions must have gotten around and trickled down to the Market vendors. Obviously, the Camps had picked up on what I was doing. Anyone tracking my purchases and watching me hustle every day could probably have figured out fairly quickly that I wasn't letting any grass grow under my feet. Thinking back now, I was likely being "prospected" by the Mob long before I was approached, without knowing it.

My assigned routine was to work four days a week in the Rochester districts, and on the other day, I drove all the way down to Elmira, where I had several clients, to service the stores and restaurants there. Soon, I was making more money than any of the other salesmen, and eventually, the company had to sit down with me and revamp their way of doing things. I was elevated to a commission-only salesman, serving as a floater; besides finding new clients, I could fill in for any position and continue to make really good money, both for myself and the produce company. They gave me a station wagon with the company logo on a magnetic, removable sign on the side. I was making fewer trips to the Farmer's Market, but was still a regular there.

But, by that time I had those three young children to support. Why hadn't I figured out what was causing that? Damn! Raising kids was an expensive proposition; in fact, it still is. So, money and the acquisition of same had replaced sex (well, almost) as my top priority in life. I was still nuts about Norma and thought she walked on water, even if working for a living kept me from showing my adoration 24/7.

Blast forward to that day when I sat there with that .45 pressed to my head. The string of events leading up to it is etched in my memory forever and is described in the next chapter.

CHAPTER THREE

I'd developed a good rapport with some of the Market vendors that I patronized. One of these was the aforementioned Joe Camp. He was a bit shorter than his brother, Alphonse, and a bit pudgier. Alphonse (aka "A.J.") looked every bit the Italian lover-- tall, dark, slim, and handsome. These two brothers, their other brother Louie, and their father, Papa Camp, were very successful produce vendors. That's how I'd come to meet them and establish rapport on a first-name basis.

One day, I was making my usual buying rounds at the Market. When I reached the Camp's stall, Joe said, "Hey, Chris, I noticed you're not driving that produce truck anymore. What's doing on?"

I told him that our company was undergoing some operational changes and how my job had changed. I added that we were now including canned goods in our product line, and Joe replied, "Yeah, I heard about that." He casually suggested that I set up a time to come by his spot at the Market and the two of us would go elsewhere to talk at our leisure. So, I arranged to stop by a few days later.

By then, I had heard more specific rumors about the Mafia's presence in Rochester, casually referred to as "the Mob," but I was still basically a naïve North Country boy and didn't really know much. Certainly, I had never heard of the powerful *Valenti* brothers other than as vendors at their stall in the Market. But, I was soon to become very well acquainted with them and many other mobsters in their formidable capacity.

When I stopped by to see Joe on the appointed day, he and I walked through the market to a large building in which the Camps had their office. (There was also a big car repair and storage garage nearby on Central Avenue that they owned, but I didn't know about that at the time.)

As I sat in their small, grimy office, chatting with Joe, A.J. came in. They both picked my brain about my sales background and experience, and I told them in detail about my role with the company where I was employed. Joe hinted at some possible work I could do with his company, and told me to come back again a couple of days later.

During that next meeting, Joe said, "Well, this is great. The business we're in could use a good driver, and we're also looking for a business partner. Do you think your boss would be interested in the business part? We'd like to make arrangements for supplying some of the stores and restaurants we manage."

I told him I'd have to ask my employer, but I suspected that Sam Fields would be just as greedily interested as I was. Little did I know then that Joe would quickly become my new main boss and teach me what *power* really was.

As we talked, a broad smile crossed Joe's face. "You sound like just the young fellow we need," he said. "Give me your work telephone number and I'll be in touch with Mr. Fields. Meanwhile, you talk with him about the produce side of things."

Joe then asked me how well I could drive a car. I probably lit up like the proverbial neon sign as I described my previous experiences driving at age 16 in stock car races and my lifelong love affair with speeding in fast cars. Joe chuckled as I described how I used to outrun the cops up in Watertown and on the back roads during my thrill-seeking teenage days. He looked me over carefully with a speculative expression. "Come on," he said, "Let's go for a drive."

We walked over to the Central Avenue garage where the Camps stored their vehicles. I saw a whole fleet of Lincolns and Cadillacs, including beautifully-outfitted limousines. Joe pointed to a particularly gorgeous, shiny black 1959 Cadillac sedan, and said, "We'll take this one." He handed me the keys.

What a beautiful car, such as I'd only dreamed of driving! I slid onto the leather seat, quickly scanning the dashboard to familiarize myself with its many features. It was incredibly comfortable, so luxurious compared to most of the older "beaters" I usually drove. The interior's smell just exuded class. My right foot found the accelerator and was itching to see what that beautiful car could do on the road.

"Go ahead, fire her up," Joe encouraged. I turned the key in the ignition and was instantly assured by the smooth purring of the big engine. Hoo-boy, was I going to have fun!

"Let's go out this way." Joe directed me to an exit that put us out onto the street. "We'll just head out over towards the airport," he continued.

As I drove, Joe asked me, "Do you know how to lose a tail? Someone who's deliberately following you like a cop--only maybe it isn't a cop?"

I thought for a moment, then replied, "Well, sure; it has to happen quickly, the same way I outran those cops in Watertown. You have to really know cars and what they can do, especially the one you're driving. Then you also have to know what that particular tailing car is capable of, and you plan to drive faster and trickier than most drivers can take it."

Joe nodded. "Exactly. And, if you normally take a regular route to a place, you need to have a Plan B and Plan C, so you can quickly deviate from that route to reach your destination without being followed. Here, let's give it a try. Don't worry about your speed here, that's not a problem. Kick it down! I want you to go like a bat out of hell. See that car behind us? Get away from it. Let's go!"

I grinned and hit the gas. We flew over the streets and took corners as though they were butter. The Cadillac responded beautifully and I was thrilled and very impressed. I wondered to myself why we hadn't attracted the attention of a cop, and also why Joe had said not to worry about the speed. For a brief moment, I also wondered who was in that tailing car that had quickly disappeared from the rear view mirror.

Most of all, though, I was acutely aware that, where I came from, that style of driving would have caught the attention of a cop from the first minute and the red lights would have been on my ass. I kept expecting some to appear—but there weren't any. How could that be?

Very soon, I would come to realize that it was part of the power that the Mob commanded. The cops were in their back pocket and knew better than to challenge them. But right then, I was still in the dark about such things. Racketeering, bribery, and corruption were just words I'd heard but not connected to anything in my sphere of experience.

Finally, Joe directed me to head back to the garage. "Let's go talk some more."

Back in the office, Joe began explaining the details of their business.

"I'm letting you in on something most people here don't know. We're a family and we frankly are involved in a lot of matters not approved of by the law. Selling produce here is just a cover."

Whoa! I did my best to keep my facial expression impassive, although my mind was starting to go on a trip of its own.

"We run a strict operation," Joe continued. "Now, I can see how a bright, ambitious young fellow like yourself could serve us well." He smiled. "We need smart, clever people here and we would certainly make it worth your while. We pay very well. One thing you'd be doing is making some special runs for us, like picking up and delivering packages containing various things. Now, the stuff might be in a produce box, but it isn't produce--and it's none of your business to know what's in there. You understand? Discretion is essential."

What could I do in reply except nod like an automaton? Good grief, I wondered, what am I about to get into?

"Our names are well-known here," Joe went on. We're part of a big family. You know the Valentis here at the Market?"

"Well, yes, I sometimes buy a couple of items from them for my company," I admitted.

"Good. Well, Stan and Frank Valenti are part of our Family. In fact, they're kind of our bosses when you come right down to it. We're all part of the *Maggadino* and *Colombo* families from Buffalo."

"Yeah, okay," I replied. Who the hell were they, I wondered?

"And you already know 'Mustache,' who often works in our stall. He does a lot of stuff around the Market in general, too."

I knew Joe was referring to a big, pudgy guy with a bushy, walrus moustache. He and I usually joked around and passed the time of day when I came in to pick up orders. But he did more than just unload produce trucks and that stuff; he kept his eyes open for cops and other people who might be threats to our guys. While he was always chomping on a big cigar, Mustache was very colorful in his use of the language; he swore a lot.

We both had our jobs to do, and that was to take care of our bosses. Mustache and I didn't like each other very much, but we could not show or act on this dislike. The Boss didn't want us fighting with people in our circle, so we made an effort to get along together as best we could.

32

Meanwhile, my mind was going a mile a minute during this conversation with Joe. What the hell were they doing at the Market exactly, besides selling fresh produce, I wondered?

"There are quite a few areas where you can be a big help," Joe added. "It's a wide range of jobs here and there. And," he stopped for a moment for emphasis, "the less you know, the better off you'll be. Got that?"

My eyes felt as big as saucers at this point, and I struggled to sound noncommittal. "Sure," was all I could muster. This was all way too much for a small-town kid like me to deal with, but at the same time, I was thrilled almost out of my shoes.

Joe talked a bit more about the job and its duties. "I also need a good, loyal bodyguard who's a clever driver and who'll get me where I need to be quickly and safely. And, we need a trustworthy, reliable man to drive my father, Papa Camp, home every day, after work."

I knew he was referring to a small, gray-haired, seventyish man who sat in the family's produce sales stall and took the customers' cash.

After a moment, Joe continued, "You'd be pressed into service for a wide range of jobs. Most of the time, you'd be packing—that means carrying a concealed weapon. We'd supply you with firearms and make sure you know how to use them. The best part of all is, you'd be paid very well; what you get from your employer now would look like chump change compared to what you'd make with us."

Guns, money, fast cars—wow! Was I having a dream or was this really happening to me? I did a quick reality check at the time, and decided that I must be living in the moment all right. But it all seemed so other-worldly to me, kind of surreal.

Then I was sitting there in the little office, with A.J. pressing that .45 to my temple and my whole world spun around 180 degrees. I was wide awake and more than a little terrified. But, as usual, my common sense had taken a hike and I decided that I was ready for the ride of my life. Hell, wasn't I invincible?

CHAPTER FOUR

When I was talking with Joe about joining the *Mafia*, I was mostly thinking about my family and what it would mean for them-- more money and a better quality of life. I never gave a thought to all of the bad things that might happen later on. Boy, was I stupid to think that everything was just about me. In the end, those guys didn't work that way and they got the better of it. But, at the time, it all sounded good to me. I wanted to give my kids everything I didn't have when I was growing up. I sure didn't count on giving up so much of my time and freedom and trust, either. Or what it really meant that I would be bound by oath and potential violence to live by their rules. Life is full of tough lessons to learn; too soon old, too late smart. Boy, is that true.

So there I was, about to learn what being a Mob associate was all about and to experience firsthand the way that the Mafia accomplished things, including corruption and racketeering.

The produce company I worked for had recently changed ownership and was carrying a lot of debt on their books. Joe already knew about that, for the next time we spoke, he brought it up.

"Yes, I've been thinking about that, too," I replied. "I told my boss that if he would turn me loose, I could do some collections."

Joe nodded in approval. "You'll need some extra manpower for that. And, you'll need these."

He laid two handguns on the table. "Like I said the other day, we'll see that you get training on how to use them. And, always remember that if you pull one of these babies out, you'd better be prepared to use it. Once that bullet leaves the barrel, you can never put it back in. Now, let's go get some lunch."

Joe, A.J. and I all headed over to the Blue Gardenia. It was a famous restaurant of considerable notoriety in Rochester. That place was also one of my produce company's customers, but I had no idea that it was actually pretty much owned and run for and by the Mob. While the majority of the customers frequenting the Blue Gardenia were mobsters or related associates, it was a popular spot for dinner among the non-criminal folk, too.

"Chris, this is Stan Valenti." Joe introduced me to a tall, well-dressed man who had a very commanding presence and voice.

Indeed, *Constenze* "Stan" Valenti's power was obvious. I was also introduced to some other men, too. Joe explained that I'd joined the team mainly as a driver and bodyguard.

"I'll give you all the help you need," Stan told me. "You want to do collections, you do it at night, with reinforcements. You won't have to get involved physically; muscle will do the dirty work."

He went on about this subject for several minutes, then Joe spoke up. "Chris is gonna be busy tomorrow getting clothes."

Stan nodded in approval, "That's good. You gotta dress the part, no shabby-looking outfits. Success gets success."

He could say that; Stan was always handsomely dressed, like a model out of a gentleman's magazine. In fact, when Stan entered a room, everyone deferred to him and made sure he wanted for nothing. He was distinguished looking as well as acutely tuned in to everything and you could just feel it. Stan Valenti was not one to blend into the woodwork; you always knew he was there. He had an indisputable presence.

Meanwhile, Joe made sure that I was going to be all right with their offer. Privately, he told me, "You don't have to do this, Chris. You can still walk away, and no hard feelings."

While I didn't actually know if there would be consequences, the look on Joe's face and in his eyes made it clear that it would not be a good idea to turn down his offer.

I shook my head. "No, I'm okay with all of it. And I'll do my very best, that's for sure."

I needed the money for my family and secretly thought it was going to be so cool to be a mobster. But it did put me at a crossroad-- to agree to their terms or to back out. It was my last chance to do the latter.

Joe added, "What you do not know or see or tell anyone will be good for you."

Hmm. That was an unmistakable message, and even though I wasn't the brightest bulb on the tree, it sure didn't seem logical for a Mob boss to share so many secrets with an outsider and then trust him to just walk away and not to brag about it to anyone who'd listen. What was the old wartime expression--"loose lips sink ships" or something like that? No, I'd better go along with it, I thought, keep my mouth shut, and damn the consequences.

"Okay, Chris," Joe smiled. "Let's get you outfitted." He picked up the telephone and made the arrangements.

After that, I was sent to get my clothes. Yes, the Mob was even going to dress me! This involved several fitting sessions with a clothing tailor, and I was carefully measured for the wardrobe of my life. There were two versions of traditional chauffeur's livery—one in a soft gray fabric, the other a formal black outfit; both included hats. They also gave me soft, leather driving gloves to match. These gloves fit beautifully and, as I would soon find, could be comfortably worn while handing a gun and even pulling the trigger. They didn't miss a thing, I concluded. Obviously, I sure wasn't the first new associate they'd outfitted, and I wouldn't be the last. But they seemed to believe in making at least an initial investment in their helpers.

"Everyday" two-piece suits, dressier three-piece suits, several tuxedos, handsome dress shirts, etc. followed, all tailored and custom-fitted just for me. There were several casual outfit items too—slacks, shirts, leather jackets. Even the underwear and socks were of the highest quality.

All of this wardrobe was stored in an exclusive special room the Mob had in a building over a bar located near their big garage. The first time I was shown into this room, I was amazed at how well-thought-out it was. Big locked closet doors all along the walls, when opened, revealed each man's entire wardrobe of clothing, hats, and other items. An overhead shelf kept the hats and chauffeur's caps handy. Storage for gloves, underwear, bow ties, and other accessories was provided by a built-in chest of drawers. Along with all of the shirts, suits, jackets, and slacks hanging there were special hangers sporting a variety of regular ties in every color and design. There was even a little pigeonhole spot on the chest of drawers where notes could be left for each "employee."

And, of course, there was a locked cabinet to hold my guns, with large supplies of ammunition for both.

At intervals along the walls of other side of the room, there were full-length mirrors and empty clothing racks, making it easy to hang a shirt and jacket on them while a guy got dressed. A couple of wheeled carts with empty bins stood ready for us to put clothing items in for cleaning or laundering. Everything was efficiently organized and easy to use. It was easy for the people in charge of the wardrobes to return items to the correct section: we each had an assigned number. Mine was "4." My clothing all bore labels with that number, and even my pigeonhole for notes was numbered accordingly.

The clothes really blew me away. For the first time in my life, I could truly appreciate the difference in how off-the-rack-or-shelf clothing just didn't have the same feel as custom-tailored, high-quality clothes. The first day when I put on the formal chauffeur's livery outfit, I stared at myself in the mirror. Boy, I would not only act the part of a mob driver and *soldier*, I would dress the part! I hardly recognized myself. They even issued me a variety of expensive wristwatches so that I would always be wearing one appropriately matched to my clothing.

Technically, I wouldn't ever be classified as a genuine *soldier*, because I'm not of Italian descent—a critical distinction with the Mob. To really classify my job would put me kind of in the middle between an *associate* and a *soldier*. I did more than the former and less than the latter. But, heck, I could carry out the part, no matter what my nationality, right? All of the guys in power treated me like any of the other *bonafide soldiers* and I was okay with that.

Various other indoctrination activities--including expert training to use a firearm—followed. After intense professional training at a local firing range, Stan Valenti offered me the use of a .45 and a .22. But Joe Camp assured him that he'd already given me the same caliber armaments. That smaller gun sat on my ankle whenever we went out together. The .45 semiautomatic was tucked into my shoulder holster where it was easy to grab when needed.

That's when I learned that I would always need to wear a jacket, even when driving Joe or his father around on a family errand. Wearing that shoulder holster, it would never do to be pulled over by a cop or spotted as I drove by one. There were no carrying permits on any of those guns; they weren't registered and had been obtained illegally. So, we didn't want to be observed or caught with them. So that's why they'd outfitted me with so many suits and also casual jackets; I always had to wear one, even on a warm day. That made me appreciate air-conditioning all the more, especially when I was driving.

Shortly after all of this fun, I was thoroughly cowed—and scared to death—on the occasion of meeting Stan Valenti's brother, Frank. That man could freeze ice in Hell with one glance, I swear. He was the real brains behind the Rochester Mob; he ran the show then, although Red Russotti eventually became the equivalent of the Godfather there in the city. Stan was very powerful, too, but in a more understated way. Frank was the more visible and aggressive of the two brothers.

And, I wasn't the only one who was afraid of him. The general attitude prevalent in the Rochester organized crime scene was, "You don't mess with Uncle Frank." I was triple-careful to give a thousand percent of my respect to him. Anyone who valued his life wouldn't have done otherwise.

At that time, I was still unaware of the Mob history involving the Camps and the Valentis. Here's a short history lesson: There had been a big Mafia event known as the Apalachin Conference. In 1957, following that conference, Stan and Frank had both been jailed for refusing to answer questions about the meeting. Then, in 1958, Stan was sentenced to 16 months in prison. During his absence Jake Russo became the new boss of the Rochester rackets. (Up to that time, Stan Valenti had been in charge.)

I know now that, in 1964, Frank Valenti had staged a violent takeover of the Rochester family. Jake Russo had conveniently "disappeared" and was never seen again. So, by the time I became acquainted with the Camps and Valentis, the power change had taken place and these guys with whom I associated were really some badass fellows!

Frank Valenti led a very colorful life. "Uncle Frank," as some folks called him, was born in 1911, and was also known by other aliases, including "Larry Costello" and "Joe Jackson." He began his criminal career in street gangs, involved in petty crimes. This included robbing gambling dens in Cleveland, Ohio. His buddies included future mob rat *Jimmy "The Weasel" Fratianno* and *Anthony DelSanter*. From 1933 on, Valenti was arrested several times for charges including assault and battery, murder, extortion, counterfeiting, and bootlegging.

Valenti became a well-earning member of the Pittsburgh crime family, then under the command of *John Sebastian LaRocca*. Then Valenti became a crew member of *Antonio Ripepi*, his brother

Stan's father-in-law (Stan was married to Catherine N. Ripepi). There is much more history to explore about Frank Valenti, but in summary, he was himself a legendary boss and founder of the Rochester crime family. He headed up that organization from 1964 until 1972. Basically, the Rochester organization was formed with help from the Pittsburgh crime family, and operated on territory established by the Buffalo crime family.

The little punks in today's street gangs brag about commanding (and demanding) respect, but those dumb little pissers flashing their gang signs can't hold a candle to the real power that the Mob had. We're talking real power here, not just a bunch of *macho* posturing and putting on airs. We were carefully trained on firearms handling. Most contemporary street gangsters simply imitate what they see and wave a handgun around indiscriminately. Half of them can't it the broad side of a barn.

The contemporary gangbangers seem to think that dealing drugs and prowling residential streets and indiscriminately using an AK-47 to spray bullets into a crowd of people makes them powerful. It's a bit reminiscent of the days of Al Capone and his famous Tommy gun. But all these young guys are doing is instilling hate among themselves and devastating the families of the innocent victims who're in the wrong place at the wrong time and die in the crossfire. Many are lone-wolf operators, who hang around with their "home boys" and a few good buddies.

When I "ran with the boys," it was so much more than just waving a gun in someone's face and saying, "You better respect me." The biggest difference between that Wild-West vigilante mentality and the Mob's organized crime activities is the power factor. Real power was about having cops look the other way while criminal activity was going on. It was about legal charges and fines quickly being dropped before a court date could be set. And, it was also about how people covertly and suddenly just "disappeared," with no one asking where they'd gone. I saw it all the time. There were a couple of guys loosely affiliated with our organization and one day, I realized I hadn't seen them for a couple of weeks. They never did appear again. Their disappearances weren't at the same time, but the result was the same--they were simply gone. No local news reports ever mentioned them and nobody in Rochester was talking. That silence told me to keep my mouth shut and my thoughts to myself.

Some of those piss-ant gangsters on the streets today openly brag about how bad they are, but most of them just wind up looking stupid. Occasionally I watch "The First 48," a popular TV show about police efforts to solve a murder within that crucial 48-hr. time frame. Over and over, I see those knuckleheads sitting there and responding to detectives' questions with, "I ain't know nothing." And that's after they've seen the damning videotape that clearly shows them holding the gun and doing the shooting! It usually turns out that they know plenty, but seem to think they can just erase what they did with their flat-out denials of what can be plainly seen on surveillance tapes.

However, I can relate to how taking an attitude of ignorance like that can sometimes be a saving grace, as you'll read later on.

Granted, the Mob "hits" from my time would have been solved much more quickly back if there'd been the on-every-corner video camera presence. They'd never have gotten away with it. Back then, though, the guys I traveled with didn't have to brag—their power and punch was already known. They were smart, always thinking, and made sure they paid off (or compromised) the cops, judges, and others who could rain on their parade.

Sure, the big conspicuous gangsters of yesteryear, including *Al Capone*, would deny their guilt right to the last, and there was so often that little shadow of a doubt that would set them free. Free, that is, until the tax evasion realities took their toll on the freedom of Capone and others.

So, don't tell me about some two-bit gangbanger or a notoriously posturing politician wielding power. I've seen real power. It's both exhilarating and terrifying and has no connection to the average person's reality.

As I recall my past life, I've often thought that several of my other Mob associates would have loved to have more power-- Mustache, especially. He, too, was kind of a wannabe like today's gangbangers, always looking for a chance to grab some power but didn't quite make the grade as *soldier*. He could play the rough-and-tough role and knew how to take and follow orders and be a muscle man, but he didn't have enough of the sharp critical thinking skills it took to make crucial, split-second decisions when they were needed.

Within a few weeks of my acceptance into the Rochester Family, I was driving Joe Camp and other mobsters around to various meetings. They had special spots in Rochester where they convened and hobnobbed with the Valentis, *Rene Piccarreto, Sammy Gingello* (known simply as Sammy G), *Thomas Didio*, and other Mob leaders. I got to know all of those other guys on a first-name basis, but when I was in public (or private) places with them, I quickly learned to just listen and not speak unless someone asked me a specific question.

Sammy G (Salvatore Gingello) was a very colorful gangland figure in Rochester's organized crime history. He was born and raised there. Having been called Sonny as a youngster, he disliked the nickname and tried to make up for it by being the toughest guy in his home neighborhood. Gang warfare in Rochester began in the early 1960's, and Sammy moved up the ranks during the middle of that decade. He became a *capo* in early 1970. Then he was involved in a scam collecting deposits for a gambling junket in Las Vegas. While he and his associates secretly kept the money, they called the police and reported it stolen. Kind of sounds like some of the scams in the news today, doesn't it?

Anyway, Sammy and family underboss Samuel Russotti blamed *William "Billy" Lupo* and used the excuse to have him murdered, as I'll discuss in a later chapter.

While we're reviewing a bit about some of the Rochester guys I ran with, Stan Valenti deserves a little attention, too. He was born in 1926, so he was 15 years younger than his notorious brother, Frank. His wife's father was Antonio Ripepi, a very powerful *capo* in the Pittsburgh crime family. This was where Frank ran the family's organization and oversaw the gambling, prostitution, and extortion rackets that spread to Rochester. That's also where he and Stan ran the wholesale produce business when I met them. In fact, in 1957, Stan was boss of the Rochester crew of the Pittsburgh crime family. I learned all of this history over time, and the power of the Valentis was not to be questioned by anyone I knew. Stan and Frank were powerful and effective and you could sense that about them even during a casual encounter for the first time.

These gangsters didn't spend their time holed up like trapped rodents. They got around and let their power be known in a social atmosphere. Restaurants and diners, including the Blue Gardenia,

Ben's Café Society, the Living Room, and Skinny's were some of our hangouts. We also frequented the establishment referred to as "the One-Eleven;" it was located at 111 East Avenue, right in the heart of the city. Regulars like Georgia Durante and other glamorous women and Mob-groupies frequented the same spots.

Incidentally, the One Eleven has recently undergone a facelift and interior remodeling. Some of the original charm has been saved and it's an attractive place now with a more contemporary appearance.

Georgia Durante was very well-known. She had been The Kodak Girl in 1960, with her pretty face and sexy body out there on billboards and other media for everyone to see. Such a lovely woman, she was the frequent eye candy and arm ornament for Sammy G, in particular. She made her mark mainly as a get-away driver and romantic interest for the guys; she wasn't into criminal stuff that I know about. Georgia was pretty notable in her proximity to Henry Hill, the famous gangster whose story was told in "Wiseguy" (Nicholas Pileggi, 1985). They actually worked on a cookbook together, which was published some time later and is still available today. She was able to move on with her life in very positive ways and is doing well today as a businessperson. Her own story was told in "The Company She Keeps," a book Georgia wrote (and that I highly recommend) after she left the environs of the Mob. It offers a woman's point of view of her association with many of the same guys I ran with, which is rare since the Mafia is a male-dominated organization.

Back in my time, the main thing I never did around Georgia and the other women favored by the Mob was to look directly at them or--worse yet--make eye contact. That would have put me in a coffin in short order! Many of those mobsters had hot tempers, were insanely jealous, and had no compunctions about shooting people just for the hell of it. Sammy G was one of those hotheads and I took care not to put myself in his or anyone else's line of fire. A.J. Camp had a similar temperament.

The equivalent of Sammy's and A.J.'s type today is those dumb street gang-bangers whose excuse for shooting someone is "because I didn't like the way he looked at me." It's not really too different than several other Mob guys I knew, when I think about it now.

What about the money? Wow, yes--the money! The cash thrown around by the Mob truly dazzled me, a simple, penny-pinching boy from the North Country. Hell, when I was young, a ten-dollar bill was like the Mint to me! In Rochester, I was frankly stunned and, at the same time, wildly impressed with the over-the-top flow of money going on between these mobsters. Thousands of dollars in cold, hard cash literally changed hands right in front of me every day. The Mob spent a lot of money on all kinds of things. The guys all carried big wads of bills and habitually forked over $100 tips for a $15 restaurant tab. Even for a simple cup of coffee, Joe would toss the waitress a $20, smile, and wave off the change.

For a small-town guy like me who'd always had to pinch pennies until they screamed, this was a great example of financial freedom and the lush life. Soon, I would be given a nice share of that cash, too. And, I would blow it just as I'd seen them do! We never learn, do we?

Speaking of money, several times during my years with "the boys," I was sent to the mayor's office to deliver a small package from my boss. Also, I'd go to the police chief's office and leave a package for him with the front desk receptionist. These packages were small and very light, and there's little doubt that they contained cash in the form of currency. Gifting cash and creating compromising situations: that's how they kept influential people and law enforcement in their back pockets.

They also spent large sums on women they paid for some of the bigwigs to have fun with. I could have any of those women for myself at no charge, according to Joe. (No, I didn't take them up on the offer.) That's one thing I will say; all of us who took good care of our bosses were, conversely, well taken care of by them.

While I was now wearing custom-tailored shirts and suits, they always remained in that Rochester wardrobe closet during my non-working hours. So, my wife, family, and friends back in our hometown never saw me looking so cool. Too bad; I was slender and good-looking, if I do say so myself. It may be a cliché that clothes make the man, but it's a true cliché. It all made me feel even more invincible, and added to my increasing sense of my own power.

Underlying that power was a lot of fear, although I never let my fear show. But, deep down, I was living a terrified double life fueled mostly by adrenaline, knowing that my life could get snuffed out in a heartbeat and wondering when it might happen. It was a wild time.

CHAPTER FIVE

We'd driven over to Skinny's for a meeting with other members of Joe's gang. They were all gamblers and other racketeers, seated at a couple of big tables in the back of the restaurant. We all had a beverage, including me, then some rivals started to drift into the restaurant. The minute the rivals began coming in the door, I jumped up and stood squarely in my usual bodyguard position directly behind Joe.

"Take it easy, Chris," he murmured. "Just keep your eyes open."

I already had unbuttoned my jacket so my gun would be easy to grab if necessary.

The newcomers brought the total "attendance" to around 20. They headed right for our tables there in the back of the room, and it wasn't long before the accusations and arguments started. A real rip-roaring territorial dispute ensued, mostly over territorial boundaries. Everyone was packing, and everybody knew that, too. It made for a very volatile situation. I was so thankful that A.J. wasn't there, because it would have turned into a real bloodbath in a hurry.

"Okay, everybody, let's all sit down and calm down!"

Joe Camp's voice carried over the others. Naturally, with everyone seated, he knew that the risk of gunfire diminished considerably; it's harder to shoot someone when you're seated.

When push came to shove, this bunch was more worried about competition than cops. If anyone from the local law enforcement ranks had walked in just then, they'd have likely been ignored. That's because this particular meeting focused tightly on the increasing territorial encroachment from other rival groups.

Suddenly, the entrance door opened again, and a particular man walked right in and headed for Joe. Instinctively, I stepped over to get between the two, but Joe beckoned the man, who moved closer and whispered something to Joe. As he did so, I felt Joe's hand patting my lower leg, which was hidden by the tablecloth. I knew that pat meant the visitor was okay and I was not to engage aggressively with him. A moment later, it was over, and the man left the restaurant. Joe got to his feet and said that we'd been called away on urgent business, and he and I hurried out to the car.

"We're going over to Batavia Downs, Chris. Take the back way, you know the route I mean. We'll meet a guy over there on the east side of the smaller parking lot, got it?"

I nodded.

"Don't call attention to us on the drive over there; just drive normally--no speeding or anything."

Driving as directed, I got us over to the famous racetrack in a few minutes. Joe had closed the glass screen separating the front and back interior seats and I could faintly hear him talking on the car phone as I drove. Naturally I was watching for a tail on the way over, but none appeared. I've always had a sixth sense about the proximity of cops and was relentless in checking out my surroundings. Remembering how my grandpa broke the rules and got away with it by using his head, I usually stayed several steps ahead of trouble.

I pulled into the designated area of the parking lot.

"That's it over there!"

Joe pointed to a big navy-blue Lincoln, and I carefully pulled up alongside so both cars faced opposite directions and the passengers could talk freely.

"Chris, keep your gun right there with you and get us out of here fast if another car comes into the lot here. We won't be more than ten or fifteen minutes." Joe instructed me as he rolled down his window.

My .45 was right beside me on the seat as the two men talked. I knew that two big dark Lincoln limos could attract attention and I checked my mirrors and windows constantly. Finally, Joe opened the glass between us and instructed me to get us out of there by a different route. I took the back roads along the 5 and 20 and eventually we got back to the Market free and clear.

While I don't know exactly who the guy was in that other Lincoln, I know that the matter concerned out-of-town (Buffalo) business. I never heard any specific gossip or chatter as to what it was all about or who was involved. Of course, it could have been discussed in some sub-language of the Mob's own "code" and I wouldn't have known what was being discussed. I was smart, but not *that* smart.

In fairness to Joe, I must say that he really protected me from the dangerous details. It kept us both safe. Stan was the same way.

Now that I've stepped back and had time to reflect on those days when I ran with the boys, I realize that neither Joe nor Stan ever deliberately exposed me to the really ugly or ruthless side of Mob life. That showed wisdom on their part; the less I knew, the less I could blab, carelessly or while under pressure. They knew they could trust me, but didn't leave room for me to buckle in weakness and give the enemy an advantage. So, all I knew that particular day was that some kind of "turf war" had been averted--at least for the time being. As a result I would live to see at least one more day, which is not usually a bad thing.

# # #

My driving skills sure came in handy and the guys took full advantage of my skill behind the wheel. One day, when I was at the Market, Joe and I took a ride over to a spot where he wanted to speak to another boss from another team. We were very careful to not be followed, but when we reached our destination, I said, "Joe, it doesn't feel right. It's too quiet and I don't like the look of this place. I'm not being funny; something's just not right." The location was a deserted parking lot near a big warehouse.

Joe had learned to respect my opinion on these matters, and he said, "Okay, let's get out of here real fast."

I turned the car around and started heading back to the market, but right at the very next corner, I saw two big black cars, one on each corner.

"Joe, get ready! We're in big trouble!"

I pulled out my .45 and put in on my lap. Joe was in the front seat and I told him to jump into the back seat, which he quickly did. Then I hit the gas and turned the car around. Joe was on the car phone by then, and he told me to see if we could keep ahead of the pursuers. I was driving really fast, so fast that I took a corner on two wheels (shade of my earlier teenage driving days!). Then I saw three or four police cars in the road right in front of us. I flew by them and hung an immediate right on the next side road, and the two cars following us were stopped by the cops. The delay made it possible for us to escape our rivals.

Once again, I marveled at the power these guys had. I didn't have that back in my freewheeling driving days in Watertown; it sure would have come in handy then.

Joe was glad to get back to the Market safely. He told Stan what a good job I'd done and how good I was at handling a car in dangerous situations.

Another time, we went to the funeral of a Mafia boss. Burial was at the big, famous Mt. Hope Cemetery in Rochester. The day was sunny and bright, much more preferable than a gray, rainy atmosphere.

Naturally, I was in my formal, dark chauffeur uniform. I was told to stay in the chauffeur role and not to leave the car unguarded for an instant, as a bomb could quickly be planted under it. Naturally, I was also advised to keep both of my guns at the ready all the time. The funeral procession, or cortege, spread out in considerable length, both ahead of and behind our limo.

There were a lot of cops and bigwig people there, several of whom seemed to be spoiling for a fight. I kept a watchful eye on anyone coming anywhere near our limo, and limited my verbal exchanges to "Hi, how's it going?" with other drivers. Mt. Hope is a huge cemetery, with all kinds of back roads and side spots that could have been used for an ambush. A lot of very famous historical people are buried there, as I learned later, including Frederick Douglass and Susan B. Anthony. So, there are always quite a few people prowling around or visiting graves.

But everything went okay and things proceeded without any major incidents. Joe returned to the car and I drove him back to the Market, where he changed clothes and went to check on how things were going in the produce stall.

I was much relieved, as trying to make a quick escape from that cemetery would have been difficult with its complicated layout. I left the limo in the garage and went up to our rooms to change my clothes. Then I got into the company station wagon and headed down to Elmira for the rest of the day.
# # #

As I said, if we behaved ourselves and did our jobs, we were treated well and rewarded for our efforts. Sometimes, that can lead to slack behavior and an entitlement mentality. This came to light when the bosses noticed that several of the other regular drivers for the Rochester organization were deliberately pushing their luck on a daily basis, breaking traffic laws right and left, parking in restricted zones, and other noncompliant stuff. They apparently thought they were invincible since they worked for the Mob, and this cocky attitude was going to result in real trouble. Stan and Joe were getting tired of having to fix so many tickets, because the more favors an organization calls in, the more it will fall under more scrutiny and place itself in a position of unwanted obligation to the authorities.

So, Joe and Stan assigned me the job of talking to those drivers in a group.

"Bark at 'em real good, Chris," Stan instructed. "Don't take any smart-ass crap from anyone. If they give you a hard time, they'll have to contend with me. Let 'em know that!"

Notes were left in the wardrobe pigeon holes calling for a meeting on a particular afternoon. When they were all assembled, I didn't mince words. First, I told them, "If you keep this up, you'll be fired, just on my word alone."

At first, I kept my face expressionless while I spoke. Then I turned up the heat, scowling at them and making my voice rough.

"Stan and Joe have had enough trouble keeping track of getting your stupid tickets fixed," I growled. "Almost every day, at least one of you jerks abuses your privilege of working for the Organization. Well, our *Bosses* have bigger fish to fry, and they especially don't like these infractions, because they call more attention to the organization than we want. That could kill us all, including you knuckleheads. Understood?"

The other drivers and nodded and promised to stop showing off. Not one of them questioned or hassled me. Naturally, this gave me more respect ,and with it, the feeling of power that was so addictive. I was in way over my head.

CHAPTER SIX

While I did wind up feeling used and somewhat abused by the Mob later on, I will say, in all fairness, that there were a lot of benefits that being with them brought. Their power and spontaneous generosity became apparent one day when I told Joe that my family and I were hosting a clambake at our house with some friends. Some of the things we'd planned to serve were currently out of season and more difficult to obtain than we'd anticipated.

"Do you have any idea where I can get the stuff?" I asked Joe.

"Whatcha got in mind, Chris?" Joe inquired. "You want clams, and what--fresh corn on the cob, usual upstate New York clambake stuff?"

I nodded, "Yes, I guess we didn't plan very well. I'm so busy that I overlooked our needs until my wife reminded me this morning. I have no idea where to get any of that stuff at this late date. "

Remember, this was back in the late 1960's, when out-of-season foodstuffs were prohibitively expensive to get for the average guy.

"Well, don't you worry Chris. We've got lots of connections." Joe chuckled. "Tell you what, I'll call a couple of suppliers I know and have them fly in the stuff you need. You want it for Friday night?"

"Yes. Wow, you mean you'd do that for me? What's it going to cost, by the way? I'll give you the money now."

I was just amazed that Joe would do such a thing for me and didn't expect to get anything for free. However, I was hoping that it wasn't going to be so expensive that I truly couldn't afford it.

"For you, Chris, nothing. It won't cost you a dime." Joe smiled. "You've done plenty of good things for us, now we can repay the favor."

I could hardly believe my good luck, and once again felt lucky to be working with such powerful men who also had a generous side.

Joe made sure he had all of the necessary information, including the number of guests expected, etc. so he could order the right quantities of the food.

Sure enough, Norma informed me, the goodies were delivered to our house early that Friday afternoon, in plenty of time for the gathering. She was quite impressed with my ability to sort of "snap my fingers" and suddenly we had everything we needed for the party.

It was really wonderful to have that kind of power in my pocket, so to speak, and the clambake was a resounding success. Our friends were astounded that we had the fresh clams, corn, etc. and wanted to know how I'd gotten them.

"Friends in high places," I joked, but shot Norma a look that she correctly interpreted to mean, "Keep your mouth shut!"

She just smiled and nodded. "Isn't that corn delicious?"

Naturally, I had made the appropriated gesture of extending an invitation to Joe out of simple courtesy, but of course he declined--with thanks.

There were other pleasant surprises and spiffs to come our way, too. Quite a few good, famous entertainers found their way to the clubs and concert halls in Rochester back then. I was a big country music fan and, as it turned out, so was Joe. That blew me away, the first time he tuned the car radio to a country station when we were out driving around.

"I love this stuff," he declared.

"Me, too!" I agreed. He genuinely loved the music, I could tell, and clearly had some favorite artists that I like, too.

One day, he asked me, "Chris, are you interested in going to see Charley Pride? He's coming into town next month."

"Oh, yeah! I really like that guy."

"Me, too. Listen, I'll snag some tickets for you and your wife and have them throw in some backstage passes, too."

"Gee, thanks, Joe! Wow, that's so generous of you."

Once again, I was being gifted with a special treat, courtesy of a Mob boss.

Over time, we received complimentary tickets to see many other entertainers, including Bill Anderson, Loretta Lynn, Lefty Frizzell, Merle Haggard, George Jones, Faron Young, and others. In each case, we were comp'd with free backstage passes and managed to meet all of those stars and get their autographs. There'll be more about that towards the end of this book.

My entire family was also treated to local-team baseball games and other sporting events. Tickets to various events appeared in my wardrobe pigeonhole with pleasing regularity. Probably the most memorable event was seeing the famous Harlem Globetrotters. My kids were so excited I thought they'd bust a gut or something, really. They laughed at the players' antics and were thrilled when some of them came over and spoke to the children during a break.

So, despite what happened later on, I will give credit where it's due. The Family did take good care of their own, and I was lucky to be included in that number. There is no shortage of memories-- good and bad--from the time I spent with them.

# # #

"We need to go pick up someone at the airport, Chris," Joe told me one morning.

"Sure," I replied. "Which car are we taking?"

"The black DeVille."

We parked at the airport parking lot. Joe and I went inside the terminal and waited for the man at the gate. As he walked into the concourse, Joe moved forward to meet him. The man had flown in from Cleveland. He was obviously an Italian, medium height, in good physical shape. We all proceeded to the terminal exit.

"Go bring the car up, Chris," Joe directed me, and I obliged, but with a little delay. They both got into the back seat of the Cadillac and we headed back towards the Market.

"What took you so long to get the car?" Joe asked.

"I felt like I was being watched. So, I checked under the car and took a good look all around before getting in and driving over to pick you up."

"Good job, Chris."

As we neared the city center, I kept watching my rear-view mirror. "Joe—we've got company!"

"See if you can lose him," Joe ordered, looking out the back window at a black Lincoln that was about a half-block behind us.

Joe asked his friend, "Are you packing?"

The man nodded.

"Good."

"Hang on, Joe, I'm going to run over to Henrietta Road, towards the landfill."

I knew that we had reinforcements there, should we need them.

We pulled up to an intersection. A fender-bender accident had just happened and two cars were pulled off to the side of the road.

"Joe, they're gaining on us! I can't get around this wreck. You guys get down on the floor—now!"

My warning was just in time. I heard a bullet or two hit the car. I drove the car up onto the sidewalk and maneuvered around the two damaged cars, then hit the street surface again and floored the gas pedal. We roared away at breakneck speed and I saw that the pursuing Lincoln had been unable to get past the wreck. Both drivers of the fender-bender had opened their doors and were standing in the street, effectively blocking the Lincoln from pursuing us. They were stuck waiting for oncoming traffic to clear.

Meanwhile, we headed directly for the landfill; I had a clear shot and wasted no time in getting there. We leaped out of the Caddy, threw the keys to a man there. "Ditch this car!" Joe ordered him. The man tossed another set of keys to Joe and we all scrambled into a big, dark blue Buick Electra and I drove us back to the Market without incident.

Both Joe and his friend told me, "Job well done! You sure know how to handle a car."

Joe got out and he and his friend went into the Market.

"Don't take your eyes off this car, Chris," Joe cautioned, as they walked away.

While waiting there, I realized how very relieved I was to have that incident behind me. Having shots fired at you when you're driving a car is extremely unnerving. I shook for a few minutes as I realized that I could have been killed.

A few minutes later, Joe and the friend from Cleveland were back, with A.J. coming along.

"Okay, Chris, let's go to the Blue Gardenia. Park out back near the kitchen door."

We all went in through the kitchen to our favorite table in the dining room. It was in a back corner.

Everyone was packing, I knew that. As they sat down, Joe ordered me to go back into the kitchen and keep an eye on the Buick.

"Don't let anyone near that car," he muttered. I nodded and did as I was told.

The others all lunched at their table. I ate standing up by the back door.

When lunch was over, I took all of them back to the Market, returned the Buick to the garage, and picked up my company station wagon. They'd all been very quiet in the car during the ride back. No one said much, but the tension was so thick you could have cut it with a knife.

As I proved myself to Joe and the others at the Market, they began entrusting me with more jobs that had increased risk. They also extended real family hospitality to me. Papa Camp and his wife shared a lovely home with Joe and his family. The elder Camps had comfortable separate quarters within the large, traditional, two-story house.

"We'd like to have you join us for a family dinner on Thursday," Joe told me one morning.

"Well, sure, thank you very much. It'll be a pleasure," I replied. I knew better than to say No and I told Norma about the invitation so she would know why my arrival home would be delayed. (Although, in retrospect, there wasn't much point in doing that.)

That Thursday evening, I drove Joe and Papa Camp to their home in Gates, a suburb west of Rochester. I'd only seen the attractive house from the outside previously. As we entered the front hall, a big staircase to the second floor was prominent. It was all tastefully decorated—not opulent but definitely not lacking in creature comforts. Joe's wife came forward to welcome me and she introduced me to the elder Mrs. Camp, Papa's wife. Both were very attractive Italian women. Papa's wife had gray hair, but I could see she'd been a real beauty in her day.

A few moments later, A.J. and his wife came through the door. He'd driven separately from the Market and picked her up on the way over to Joe's home. They all extended every possible gesture of hospitality to me, and I tried to relax and not be overwhelmed.

It wasn't long before I was ushered into the lovely formal dining room with a big table that could easily and comfortably seat ten or more for a big, sit-down dinner, and probably more for a large buffet. Joe had me sit next to him so we could converse easily, and he tried to put me at my ease. Quietly, as he poured wine into my glass, Joe murmured, "This wine isn't probably your kind of thing, and you needn't drink it all. Just take a sip when we do a toast."

The meal was very bountiful and traditionally Italian, from the homemade bread down to the meatballs, sausages, spaghetti, and salad. Cannoli and coffee made for a tasty dessert. I followed Joe's suggestion about the wine; he was right, it wasn't to my taste. Nobody else seemed to notice, since I raised my glass at the right time and made sure they saw me take a sip; all went well.

Afterwards, the men all retreated to the home's library, a very comfortable room lined with bookcases. It sported an attractive fireplace, which added to the masculine atmosphere. We smoked cigars and had more coffee. The others all had glasses of brandy or other liquor, but I quietly stuck to soft drinks since I had to drive home later.

Most of the time, the conversations were in English, but a few times A.J. and Papa lapsed into Italian. I could tell when they were arguing by the inflection and volume of their voices, along with expressive hand gestures. After about an hour, Joe gave me his characteristic high sign, and I knew it was time to leave. I thanked them profusely, making it a point to compliment the women on the excellent meal. Then I made my exit to drive back to the garage in Rochester to retrieve my own vehicle and drive home.

As it turned out, this was just the first of many meals which to which I was invited at the Camp home. However, Norma was never invited. Joe preferred not to mix my home life with the role in his business life, and I understood that.

However, there was one exception. I went to get something out of my "Rochester wardrobe," as I thought of it, and there was a heavy, cream-colored envelope in the pigeonhole. "Chris and Wife" was neatly inscribed on the front--that's all.

I opened the envelope and found a second one inside containing a fancy, engraved wedding invitation. It was for *Dario Ricci,* one of Stan's soldiers, who was marrying *Elena Moretti*, in a ceremony at a big Catholic church in Rochester. A fancy reception was to follow at Logan's Party House.

Formal attire was required, of course; it was to be an 11:00 a.m. wedding on a Saturday six weeks hence.

When I next saw Joe, I mentioned the invitation and the RSVP request. "Who should I contact about it?"

"All taken care of; you'll be there, no choice. I don't want you far from me at these gatherings. You don't need to wear a tux, but one of the nice, dark suits will be fine. Your wife should be in a long dress, okay?"

"Sure, Joe. What about a wedding gift, what would be appropriate?" I asked.

Joe waved it off. "That's taken care of, too. The Organization will give them something as a group. Just bring yourselves. Stop by to change into your suit on the way there. I'll wait for you in a limo at the curb. You come to me there."

I knew he meant I wasn't to take home a suit, but to go into my Rochester Wardrobe for it on the morning of the wedding. And, that someone else would be driving Joe to and from the event so Norma and I could ride in our own car.

When I showed the invitation to Norma that night, she raised her eyebrows and then frowned. "What on earth shall I wear to this?"

"Tell you what," I answered, pulling out my wallet. "Here's $200. Go out and find yourself a long dress that you'll be comfortable in. Remember that gold jewelry set I bought you in Florida? That should look nice. It's fancy enough but not gaudy."

"Oh, yeah. Okay, I'll go see what I can find. We've got six week, so I should have time to find a nice dress. I think I already have shoes that will work. What about you? Do you need a new suit?"

I knew she was mentally reviewing my meager wardrobe there at home.

"No way!" I laughed. "I have great clothes in Rochester. We'll have to stop by there so I can change into a good suit, on our way to the church."

"Why not just bring it home with you the night before?"

I shook my head. "No way. That's not an okay thing to do. Those clothes have to stay in Rochester, with few exceptions, and this isn't one of them."

Norma shrugged. "Okay by me, I guess."

On the morning of the wedding, we allowed enough time for the drive to include making my clothing change. I pulled up in front of the building in Rochester and told Norma to wait.

"I'll be right back," I emphasized. "Don't go anywhere and don't be nervous. There's nothing going on around here this morning. Everybody'll be going to the wedding."

I ran upstairs, grabbed my best dark suit, put an appropriate tie with it, and went to dress in front of one of the big mirrors. Satisfied that I was all put together properly, I tucked my .45 into its shoulder holster and also strapped the little .22 onto my ankle. Then I went downstairs and returned to the car.

"Wow, look at you!" Norma gasped. "What a nice suit, and I like that tie."

I grinned. "Yeah, I dress up real nice, don't I? You look really great in that dress and jewelry." I complimented her.

Norma had found a pretty chiffon gown in a shade of pale pink that didn't stand out more than other women's outfits. The gold jewelry I'd given her provided just the right touch of what's now referred to as "bling" but it didn't scream for attention like some jewelry does.

We drove to the big Catholic church. I don't recall which one it was, but its exterior was of classic cathedral design and it was immense and awesome inside. Of course, I had never been in such a church before, so it was all quite impressive to this ol' North Country boy.

Joe was waiting in a limo at the curb, just as he'd described, and he waved to me. I walked over to help his wife out of the car, and I introduced them to Norma as we went up the church steps. Inside, ushers showed us to our seats. I was seated directly behind Joe, and Norma was behind his wife.

It looked like the "who's who" of Rochester was all there. I recognized many local bigwigs as well as other Mob Bosses and their bodyguards. But Stan wasn't there, at least not that I saw.

Such flowers as there were in that huge sanctuary! It looked to me as though the entire contents of several florists had been collected to decorate the space.

The guests chatted quietly with one another until the organ music stopped momentarily, signaling everyone to be quiet. Then the familiar strains of the Wedding March began, and we all stood as one and looked to the back of the sanctuary. Several bridal attendants, all garbed in long, matching gowns, began to pace down the aisle, followed by a cute little flower girl and a solemn young boy carrying a pillow with the wedding rings. There was a slight pause and then we watched as a lovely Italian girl, in a gown with a long lace train spreading out behind her, came along on the arm of her father.

As they reached the wedding party spread out in front of the altar, I thought to myself that it must be wonderful to get married with money being no object. Norma and I hadn't been married in a church and there'd been no flowers other than a corsage pinned on her dress. Oh, well.

"Look at that gown," Norma whispered. "Lace on satin, and white roses in her bouquet. Wow!"

After the ceremony, the bridal couple went down the front steps of the church. Professional photographers were positioned all around, with cameras flashing as we all tossed rice into the air. Then we went to our cars and headed over to the reception.

Logan's Party House was a popular venue for hosting big parties. Norma walked in with Joe's wife, while I stayed close by him. The women murmured about the big room's decor, always attractive but today, it was festooned with more flowers than I could imagine. The covered tables all had lovely floral arrangements and were set with good china, silver, and glassware.

A small music stand in a corner held the band, which played a mixture of jazz and popular music.

The meal was spectacular; no expense had been spared. We had a menu from which to choose our entrees and side dishes. Naturally, we selected the prime rib and it was not disappointing. Joe and his wife sat at our table with several other couples, so I was able to keep an eye on who was near him. We all chatted back and forth and it was a pleasant meal, although part of me was always on guard and watchful.

At some point, I looked up and saw Stan and his wife going over to the table where the wedding party was seated. They stayed for about thirty minutes, then left right after coffee and dessert were served. Then the band switched to playing popular show tunes and other dance music. Norma's foot was tapping and she was obviously dying to dance. Joe signaled to me, "Go ahead," and I led Norma out on the floor for a slow waltz.

As I held her close, she whispered, "God, I can feel your gun against my tits!" Naturally she could feel its bulk, hidden by my suit jacket. I'd never worn it before when we danced and it was a new discovery for her.

"Don't talk about it," I whispered back.

I said that to her partly because I worried about being overheard, and partly because just thinking about her tits would give me a hard-on and that would not be good, given the situation. Then I winked at her, and she figured it out.

"Okay, I won't," Norma smiled and we finished the dance and returned to our table. A short time later, Joe gave me the high sign, and we began to say our goodbyes. The bride and groom had done their wedding dance and were far across the room, laughing and toasting each other with family members and friends.

I accompanied Joe to their table, where we both wished the bridal couple much happiness and thanked them for including us in the festivities. Then we collected our wives and left the party.

Norma and I drove back over to the building near the Market and I ran upstairs and changed out of the good suit. I carefully folded it and laid it in the bin designated for dry cleaning service. Then I got back into my street clothes and we went home.

CHAPTER SEVEN

Unfortunately, not every day could end on a nice note, and many of them sure didn't start that way, either. One morning, I was sitting in Joe's office and he got a telephone call. I started to get up and leave, but he immediately signaled me to remain in the room. A moment later, he hung up and said, "Chris, we gotta go, right now. Hurry! We'll grab the white Caddy."

I knew he meant the beautiful 1968 Fleetwood Brougham sitting in the garage. We hurried, all right, and a couple of minutes later, I stomped on the accelerator of that Cadillac as we roared out of the garage. I could vaguely hear Joe speaking urgently on the car phone in the back seat. (A glass screen separated the front and back seats.) Then his voice burst in over on the intercom speaker in the dashboard.

"Chris, take me to Main Street over at the corner of Chestnut. Drop me off there, go around the block twice real fast, and come back and pick me up!"

As we flew over the downtown city streets of Rochester, Joe was on the car phone constantly. I was again amazed that there was no police response, because I had the gas pedal down to the floor of that Cadillac. In fact, when I saw cops standing at major intersections, they actually turned their backs as we whizzed by. Obviously, word had got out that we'd be coming through and they'd been told to literally "look the other way." Now, that's power! Local law enforcement officers were in the Mob's back pockets, that much was obvious.

At the appointed corner, Joe stepped out of the Cadillac and waved me off. He disappeared into the building as I hastily drove down the block and did the prescribed circling routine twice, roaring around the corners. When I came back around the second time, Joe was striding from the building—not running, but walking at a brisk pace. He got to the car door as I pulled up to the curb, and got in.

"Put the right foot to the floor and don't stop for anything!" he ordered me.

When we had put some distance between us and where we'd been, Joe visibly relaxed. "Well," he said. "That's all right now. Thanks, Chris. Let's go get some lunch."   Joe directed me to drive to Skinny's, that popular diner where a couple of his chums were waiting. We all had lunch together. Although the conversation was low-key, I could feel some unspoken tension and a sense that something important had happened. But, no one said anything to me and later on, I dropped Joe off at his office.

The next morning, when I arrived at the Market, groups of the "regulars" had their heads together, talking about something.

"What's going on?" I asked. Someone muttered, "So-and-so was 'offed' yesterday. He was shot over in the center of town on Main in an office building."

I gulped and thought fast. That location was where I'd taken Joe yesterday. Had he killed someone while I drove around the block? Was that why speed was so essential? I knew that Joe was always packing, with his .45 semiautomatic within easy reach. Keeping my face expressionless and not reacting to the discussions, I engaged in normal conversation and then went to the Camp and Valenti vending stalls to pick up my produce orders.

"Hey, Chris, let's grab some coffee before you go on your delivery run. Stan's going to join us." Joe grabbed his suit coat.

We all walked over to Amico's, a favorite spot for coffee there at the Market. After ordering, we just sat there shooting the breeze, not talking about anything important.

Someone at a nearby table hollered, "Hey Stan, did you hear what happened yesterday?"

Stan Valenti's facial expression never changed; he was very cold and ignored the interrupters. Joe just smiled and waved to them, "Good morning," but didn't join the discussions. Then he gave me a look; it was subtle, but I interpreted it to mean, "Did you see anything, Chris? What do you know about it?"

I sensed that I was being tested as to my integrity about keeping my mouth shut, so I shrugged and feigned ignorance. "Huh. I guess something happened, but I don't really know. Actually," I deliberately grimaced, "I'm kind of distracted about that huge order for potatoes and French fries from Billy's Kitchen. I think the cook is off his chump and has no idea what he's doing." I rolled my eyes. "Sometimes those guys are just idiots when it comes to ordering. Got any ideas?"

Joe and Stan both laughed. "Good boy, Chris. You stick to your job and you'll go places. Don't worry, that guy at Billy's is always a little strange, but he pays his debts on time—"

We were interrupted by Joe the Banana Man. "I need to see you back at the stall." He directed his comment to Joe Camp, jerking his thumb backwards towards the Market interior.

"Sure, Joe, we're just going back there now."

We finished our coffee and walked out. Whew! I'd literally dodged the bullet on that one. It was yet another reminder to remain as ignorant as possible of reality.

Some time later, though, as I looked back at those days with "the boys," I learned that some of the most mysterious disappearances and actual slayings of some gangland figures had never been resolved. *Samuel C. Russoti*, a nephew of Frank Valenti's reputed *consiglieri,* and *Enrico Visconte*, were two of them. The latter was a low-level crime figure and no motive for his death was found.

However, William "Billy" Lupo was clearly linked with the upper echelon of the Rochester Mob, and he was blatantly murdered. I discussed this a bit earlier in the book. In fact, the investigation into Lupo's murder was one of the factors that brought Frank Valenti and his cronies to the full attention of law enforcement.

While I cannot swear for certain, I strongly suspect that Billy Lupo was the victim that day when I drove Stan to the spot where someone was killed. Whether or not Joe was the one who shot Billy (who was actually found slumped behind the wheel of his car), I'll never know. Modern forensics can usually establish rather quickly whether a body was moved after death, but I'm not sure if that could easily be determined back in 1970. So, the man could have been shot inside the building and then moved to the vehicle later. A lot of very volatile stuff was happening in Rochester in the early 1970's, and I'm probably very lucky that I got out when I did. Oops, I'm jumping the gun a bit here, pardon the pun. Bear with me.

Have you ever experienced one of those times when your life suddenly passes before your eyes? My knees quavered a little as I recalled that wild drive, as I realized again how close I'd come to being involved in a mob shoot-out. Because that's what almost occurred; it just happened that Joe was faster with his gun than the other guy. Mob shoot-outs weren't my favorite thing, not--pardon the pun--by a long shot. My mind immediately flew back to that first day when I pledged my loyalty to the mob with a pistol held to my head and A.J.'s words ringing in my ears.

Simultaneously, the thought of my wife and three kids waiting at home for me formed a vivid picture in my mind. I could see all those trusting pairs of eyes focused on me and feel their arms around my neck, begging to know, "When will you be home, Daddy?"

"Keep your head down and your mouth shut" wasn't a bad motto to live by. At least it gave you a fighting chance.

For mob aficionados and historians who've studied the activities of crime syndicates and bosses, this incident and following shoot-up was rather reminiscent of the start of the *Castellammarese* War. It wasn't quite as dramatic and violent as the famed St. Valentine's Day Massacre, but it wasn't too far behind, either.

Once again, for the umpteenth time, I wondered if there *would* be a "next time."

Whatever happened, it didn't affect my pay. That evening, when I was preparing to take Papa Camp home, Joe placed an envelope into my hand and winked. "Good work, Chris," he said casually. I stuck the envelope in my inside suit coat pocket.

Later that night, when I pulled into my driveway, I peeked into that envelope. Once again, there were several one-hundred dollar bills inside—my reward for the risky work and keeping my mouth shut. Not bad for a couple day's work and having nearly pissed my pants in fear.

Yes, I had to admit it: Underlying that power was a lot of fear, although I never let my fear show. But, deep down, I was living a terrified double life fueled mostly by adrenaline, knowing that my life could get snuffed out in a heartbeat and wondering when it might happen. It was a wild time.

CHAPTER EIGHT

Many days, I felt like I was running in place. There was the intrigue of danger and big money in my dealings with the Mob, and then there were the everyday demands of my job in the produce sales business.

One of the biggest sellers we carried was ready-cut potatoes for French fries. Having them all ready for dropping into a deep-fat fryer saved the restaurants a lot of valuable time in food-prep labor. After being cut, the potatoes were kept in a preservative solution within the plastic bags in which they were sold. One of our big customers in the summer, especially, was Sea Breeze. I delivered a many as 60-80 thirty-pound bags of those potatoes each week to them. The amusement park hosted thousands of people each day, and they were all hungry for the hot dogs (we just call 'em *hots*) and burgers that begged for a big pile of fries to be served with them. It takes a lot of energy to have fun and food fuels that energy; ask any kid hopping on and off amusement rides or going down a water slide.

I didn't mind the frequent deliveries; more sales meant more money in my pocket. Interestingly, the Rochester Mob didn't hold any financial interest in Sea Breeze that I knew of.

My workload, though hectic and demanding, would have been bearable. But my family life was starting to fray at the edges. Sex had more or less run my life in previous years; now it was starting to ruin it.

I was working long hours between my regular produce sales job and "running with the boys." While Norma enjoyed the increase in money I was bringing home, she was showing signs of being dissatisfied with our life. The most upsetting was that there were disturbing clues that she was unfaithful to me.

Norma had recently taken a newspaper delivery job for extra income, which required her drive around in the early afternoon, dropping off papers at various distribution points around the area. There were rumors about her and Howard Foster, a male coworker, being repeatedly seen parked out on a back road, but I brushed them off as inconsequential. That was just a standard paper-trading stop—it had to be! She was the love of my life, or so I thought, and I just didn't want to think about her screwing someone else.

We often don't see what we don't want to see and don't think about the long-term consequences of our actions. I was no different than many others who've faced similar situations--the ol' ostrich with his head in the sand. On the other hand, was it so unusual after all? Should I have been jealous—or suspicious? It was, after all, the era of "Sex and the Swinging Sixties." And I had unwittingly greased the skids for this growing trend of marital infidelity in my own backyard.

About a year before I joined the Mob, Norma and I had thought it might be fun to dip our toes into that naughty pool of rampant sexual experimentation—to a point. So, naïve backwoods nitwit that I was, when some other couples suggested that we get together for a game of strip poker, I said, "Sure."

Why not enjoy something like sex to the fullest? While the new relaxed sexual culture beckoned to my normal red-blooded male instincts, it literally hollered in high volume to Norma. We were part of the new sexual revolution, when women were finally emancipated sexually. I was shocked and amazed—and also pleased--at how fast my wife got into it. When the games began, she wasn't a particularly good poker player to begin with, so she lost her clothing quickly. Moreover, she soon took obvious pleasure in removing it as fast as possible. I'd never realized what an exhibitionist she was. She didn't stint on wearing the sexiest underwear, either, compared to the other women at the parties.

 Also, she actually encouraged the other men to play with her tits and other parts of her anatomy and damned foolish me, I didn't object. What a nitwit! Instead, I was so proud of having such a sexy wife and kind of secretly got off, in a kinky way, watching my best male friend tweaking Norma's pointy nipples. Not to be outdone, of course, I did some touchy-feely stuff with the other women, too. Norma didn't care; in fact, no one objected to any of it. We stopped short of having actual intercourse there with the others, but boy, were things hot when we got home!

From then on, Norma would fuck like a mink every night and whenever we had a few moments. She was hot to trot, now fully aware of the fun and pleasures of sex and she wanted it all the time. The sex we had after those poker games was incredible! Norma just couldn't get enough, no matter how many orgasms she had. She was always ready to initiate sex with me (and, unfortunately, anyone in pants, as I learned later).

But, at the time, I thought this was just great and I encouraged her to dress provocatively and flaunt her body, because I innocently thought she want to do it for me just to excite me for later fun and games. That's what she always said when I questioned the way she displayed her body. Since it all made me hornier than a bitch, I was always eager to grab a piece of ass whenever possible.

How easy it is to put suspicions and common sense aside when hot pussy is waiting for you! (Remember, too, I was madly in love with the woman and naively thought she could do no wrong, so this situation was living proof that love can really skew one's judgment.)

No doubt; I was an idiot. That was to become clear before long. What man in his right mind would take pride in seeing other men disrobing his wife and playing with her tits and other body parts right in front of him and other people? Why didn't it occur to me that Norma might not always wait for me to be there to have herself some fun?

When I finally woke up to what was happening, it was way too late. I learned, very painfully, that there's a difference between acknowledging one's need for sex in your life and allowing sex to stampede you into making really stupid choices. That's what it did to me—and to Norma, although she'd never admit it. Talk about too soon old, too late smart; that was me.

CHAPTER NINE

While some days in my years with the Rochester Mob were more different than others, I was usually fairly clear as to what was expected of me. That didn't mean that I fully understood or was aware of all the undercurrents going on behind the scenes. But, I seemed to be living up to Joe's expectations as far as my driving and protective abilities went; I'd gained his trust. And the Valenti brothers both approved of me, too, that much I realized. They spoke cordially to me, complimented me on my successes, and soon I was reporting to Stan almost as much as to Joe.

Some days were relatively uneventful. I'd arrive at the office and Joe would instruct me, "This morning, I need to go to out. We'll take Main Street over to Clinton and go over to John B's. I don't expect to be followed, but be on the lookout, as usual."

Most days, there was no "tail," and the errands were just routine. Then came the first day when I could tell we were being followed. I was driving Papa Camp home late in the afternoon, and in my mirror, I saw a big, dark Oldsmobile about a block behind us. I kept an eye on it. Three blocks later, it was still there, and after I made a right-hand turn, it continued to follow us. There was no doubt about it; we had a potential problem.

I picked up the car intercom microphone and tersely instructed Papa, "Hang on, Mr. Camp! Lie down on the seat. We've got someone sticking behind us and I'm going to lose them!"

Papa Camp immediately dropped flat as instructed. I boarded the Lincoln and made a series of evasive turns and bursts of speed that most drivers couldn't possibly follow. I kept this up for several miles, doubling back on our route and then looping around on side streets. After a few minutes, I knew I'd lost them, and told Papa Camp he could sit up again.

He signaled his understanding and said, in his heavy Italian accent, "Thank you." We continued to his home without incident and I made sure no one was following me as I went back to the garage near the Market. I never drove any of the Mob cars home, and the produce business station wagon didn't gather much attention. I wasn't allowed to take my firearms home, either, so I had no weaponry if I got waylaid. Thank goodness I never did.

One thing I never had to worry about was getting a speeding ticket. The traffic-ticket fixing scam was big with the Mob. But one day, Joe mentioned to me that another driver from my employer's company kept parking in the same off-limits space at the market. Each time, the ticket quietly went away, but "Doesn't he ever learn?" Joe wanted to know. "This puts a strain on things. Occasional is okay, but every week the jerk keeps parking in the same spot and gets another ticket that we have to fix."

"I'll take care of it, Joe," I replied. "I'll be seeing that guy later this afternoon back at the plant and I'll tell him to knock it off now or he'll regret it."

"Thataboy," Joe smiled. "I know I can count on you."

I did give that other driver holy hell and he got the message.

"Look, Charlie, you've gotta stop parking in that restricted space at the Market! Joe's getting tired of having to deal with fixing your weekly parking tickets, and if you don't change your ways, somebody's going to regret it--and it won't be me. D'ya get my drift?" I scowled at Charlie.

Charlie opened his mouth and started to say something, then swallowed his words. "Got it," was his response. He never parked in that space again.

Joe was pleased and let me know it in his own way. Some extra cash and a little more power were accorded to me, and I soaked it up like a sponge. Charlie and others at the produce plant started showing me more deference and respect. My own reputation was starting to precede me, which only added to my erroneous sense of invincibility.

# # #

One day, Joe mentioned, "I need to go to Buffalo tomorrow, Chris. Will that work with your schedule?"

I quickly did a mental review of my usual runs, and replied, "Sure, no problem. What time do you want to leave?"

"Let's plan to head out by 9:00. That should give us plenty of time to get over there for a lunch meeting at noon, and then get back here before the close of business."

"Deal." I shook hands with Joe and went off to make my usual calls.

The drive to Buffalo the next morning was uneventful. Joe and I passed the time chatting about produce prices and other business stuff. When we neared the city, Joe directed me to a particular off-ramp from Hwy 104. We wound up at a big restaurant, and went into its lounge. I wondered why Joe hadn't reserved one of the banquet rooms for the meeting, but he evidently felt safe enough and not concerned about privacy.

We were joined by two other men from the Buffalo Mob. The organization had huge gambling interests and activities in Buffalo back then, run mainly by the Maggadino family. The Rochester 'subgroup" was looking to expand its operations and the two groups worked together closely back then.

If memory serves, the two men who joined us were *Joseph Fino* and *Ray Carlisi*. I was invited to sit and eat lunch with them and Joe, but I wasn't included in the discussions, which focused on various racketeering activities. I listened to them talk about prostitution, gambling, shakedowns, and other illegal activities as casually as one might discuss the weather with friends. It sounded very profitable as they bragged about successes and also trotted out some fresh ideas for improving the takings.

Of course, I feigned disinterest and showed no reaction to what was being said. It was my rare chance to eat and enjoy a real lunch at my leisure. And, I resisted the temptation to jump in with ideas or questions. I may have been slow-witted in some parts of my life, but not in this realm. Being ignorant was my salvation and I knew it. This is where I can relate to today's gangbangers with their standard reply to questions, "I ain't know nothing." I kept my mouth shut and minded my own business.

We got back to the Rochester Market later that afternoon without incident. In fact, I actually had time to make a couple of sale calls before heading home for the night. That netted me another new customer, which was always good.

Some other days, I was directed to deliver packages. The usual destination was an area landfill. That sounds weird, and it's interesting how the Mob and the waste management industry are usually hand in glove. That's been true for many decades and likely it still is. Anyway, I'd first back my company station wagon up to a door near the Camps' office at the Market, and someone would appear with a large carton of what appeared to be lettuce or some other produce item. Sometimes it was heavier than other times. I could tell by the "thunk" when it was loaded into the car.

I'd start the engine and drive off towards the landfill. Sometimes, I'd really be tempted to pull off onto a side street somewhere and peek into the carton. But, the Mob had eyes everywhere and who knew if I was being watched? No, it was better that I minded my own business. No one ever opened one of those cartons in front of me, and I was sure there was some way that tampering on my part would have been evident. The fear of being caught was a strong deterrent to sneaking a peek. These were more of those times where it was what I didn't know that kept me alive.

When I arrived at the landfill, several guys were waiting. They opened the back of the car and quickly removed the carton, and I drove away without hesitation. I'm absolutely sure now, as I suspected then, that I was ferrying drugs, money, and guns.

On one particular day, I was carrying large crates of lettuce and cabbage in the company wagon, on my way to that landfill. I hadn't had to load them up myself, but I could tell that they were especially heavy by the way the guys had hefted them into the back of the station wagon. It had taken 2-3 guys to handle each box. They had to have been full of heavy guns, which the Mob needed, and hiding them at the landfill was a smart strategy.

As I drove out on West Henrietta Road, towards the landfill, I saw cops standing in the road up ahead. Their cars were parked on the road's edge. Oh, great, it was a roadblock for routine checks. The NY State cops and local jurisdictions, including the Rochester police, did that several times a year. They would stop each vehicle and check drivers' licenses, vehicle registration papers, tire condition, etc.

As I pulled my company station wagon up in line, an officer stuck his face in the window. He asked me where I was headed.

"Over to a restaurant and bar near the airport," I lied.

I was geographically pretty close to the airport by then and we actually did service several establishments there, so it was a plausible reason. But I didn't name a specific business. And I sure as hell didn't mention the landfill.

"What's in the back there?" The cop asked.

"Cases of produce I'm delivering," I replied. "Lettuce and stuff. Do you want me to unlock the back?"

I was sweating bricks inside, but stayed calm. Maybe he wouldn't ask me to open the crates.

"Yeah, open it up," he ordered.

I got out of the car and complied.

As I opened that door, I could see that somebody had planned for this eventuality, just in case. Little fragments of lettuce and cabbage lay scattered accidentally-on-purpose on top of the boxes, and each vent-hole in the crate was filled by a ball of green lettuce or cabbage. Whoever had packed the shipments had evidently put the real cargo inside a wall of vegetable product, and I knew that if the cop ordered me to open one of the crates, all he would see was the produce.

I looked at the officer questioningly, and he hesitated just a second, then said, "Okay, you're good to go!"

As I pulled away from the roadblock, I realized that I'd been really lucky to have escaped further scrutiny, and with great relief, I pulled into the entrance to the landfill a few minutes later. The guys there got the boxes out of the back and said nothing and I drove away.

When I returned to the Market, and told Joe about it, he looked pleased. "Good job as usual, Chris."

He handed me the usual envelope, and for the first time, I didn't feel guilty in taking the money. As far as I was concerned, I'd earned it. Now I was free to go make my sales calls and deliveries for my employer's produce customers.

Thinking of "other" tasks, there was also some kind of covert exchange system going on that involved briefcases. I'd be instructed to retrieve a briefcase from Stan's office and take it to someone at the landfill. On occasion, I'd take it instead to an establishment such as Marshall's Steak House, where someone would carry it to a back room and then bring out a heavier, identical briefcase, which I would leave in Stan's office when I returned to the market.

The weight of the briefcases varied and I knew there had to be something "interesting" in them. Again, though, I never peeked. They were locked, anyway, and the only keys I ever carried were to a couple of the cars in the garage.

In retrospect, some of the things going on here would appear to be taken straight from Mario Puzo's famous book, "The Godfather." That's because certain activities, actions, and behavioral patterns involving organized crime repeat themselves many times over and over again. The more I got into it, the more I realized this to be a fact.

One morning, I was on the job, with my regular produce company work. First, I had to stop at the Market for product.

Joe greeted me, and then said he needed me to make a run to a place near Buffalo to pick up some boxes of oranges and lemons and bring them back to the Market.

Privately, I thought this was odd, because the Camps always got those items directly from dealers in Georgia or Florida. But I said, "Okay, I can do that. Are you coming along? Should I take one of your company cars?"

"No, I've got stuff to do here. If you'd take your company produce car, it will look like you're making a new sales call. Oh, and be sure to take along one of your price lists and give it to the person in charge there."

So, I knew I wasn't just picking up produce. Well, the less I knew, the better.

I drove to Buffalo and met a guy named Pete at his warehouse. He showed me around the stacked boxes of produce and other items.

"Chris, why don't you pull your car inside, over here," Pete indicated a spot to the left of the big warehouse doors. "My boys will load it up for us. I'm taking you to lunch while they do that."

We walked across the street to a diner and ate. When we returned to the warehouse, the car had been loaded and was ready for me.

"I'm sure Joe is going to be very happy with the quality of these," Pete told me. "Uh, I suggest that you drive back to Rochester carefully and don't get stopped by the police."

That made me really curious about what was in those produce boxes, but, as always, I resisted the temptation to look. I drove carefully back to the Market, and got the car unloaded so I could get on with my own business for the day.

CHAPTER TEN

So many characters I met during this time were questionable at best and scary at worse. Part of my job was to always be alert and watchful of who was in proximity to who. Readers of Mario Puzo's aforementioned book may recall the incident where Michael Corleone sets up a meeting in a restaurant. The police chief and another bigwig were then unexpectedly murdered--literally blown away--when Michael came out of the bathroom with a gun that had previously been planted there for his use. That shooting initiated an intense and lengthy war between the gangs and law enforcement, a bloody reality that did take place in real life. The book was just good documentation of a slice of Mob history.

Situations such as that slyly-planned shooting were classic set-ups that I was expected to anticipate and thwart. One day, Joe, A.J. and I had all driven to the Blue Gardenia together in one car. We were there for a pre-arranged meeting with some specific people. A few moments after we'd been seated, Nature called me rather urgently and I excused myself momentarily to go to the restroom. Other people were filtering in while I was gone. While this left my boss unattended for just a couple of minutes, it came close to causing a disaster.

A.J. was watching the door during my absence, and the waiter was acting suspiciously. His behavior made A.J. uncomfortable, so A.J. said something to the restaurant owner, who told him that the man was a cousin of the regular waiter who was "out sick." While I was still in the bathroom, a rival group entered the restaurant and was seated fairly close to us.

Suddenly, A.J. knocked over a serving cart on purpose for distraction. At the same moment, the *ersatz* waiter was carrying a covered tray over to the table of the rival group from the other side of town. In the confusion, A.J. jumped him, and a gun fell from the spilled tray. Joe rose up, holding a gun and stood over the waiter, who lay on the floor, shaking in terror. The man was removed from the restaurant; Joe personally took him outside to let his henchmen deal with the man.

Joe and I met with the Blue Gardenia owner in his office after the incident. Joe told him, "If you knew about this ahead of time, you're dead!" The owner steadfastly denied having known anything about it, and Joe let him off with a deadly growl and a warning look.

As we all sat down at the table again, Joe growled at me, "No bathroom breaks allowed! Don't you ever do that again, leaving me alone like that! I'm not trying to be nasty, but I don't like feeling that vulnerable."

I felt like saying, "Well, A.J. was here all the time, and he's always ready to shoot someone," but I held my tongue and pondered the situation.

After being dressed down on that occasion for my "negligence," it occurred to me that perhaps not everyone should ride together in one car on these jaunts. For one thing, it added too much weight to the vehicle if a fast getaway was needed, and also it upped the odds that a whole group could be taken out at once if there was a confrontation. I put forth this theory and Joe instantly agreed that a change should be made. From then on, several vehicles were used to ferry the guys around to any important meetings, with each car carrying only one or two men beside myself. Something positive had come from a touchy incident and I learned a lesson I'd never forget.

Our usual waiter at the Blue Gardenia was never seen there again, although Joe and I would return there many times.   That was another mysterious disappearance which didn't go unnoticed, but it also wasn't ever mentioned.

On another day, at a Seven-Ten Club lunch, Joe was to meet someone from the other side of town. He didn't feel that things were right and told me, "Get me out of here now--and have your piece ready."

We went out the side door and saw no one. Nothing happened, but the tension was high. I had the distinct impression that the situation had everything to do with racketeering rivalry and that we somehow had dodged a bullet or at least a very volatile confrontation.

In another incident, we were trapped inside a restaurant, after dark, by a rival gang. A big group of us had met up at the 700 Club in Rochester. We got word that some rivals were close by. The car used by Joe and me was parked right out in front of the building, so we couldn't get to it safely. So, he and I had to run out the back door into an alley and take cover behind garbage cans and dumpsters.

We could hear footsteps and muttering, then the lead started flying. The whole thing really smacked of a Western outlaw movie, with bullets zinging off the metal garbage containers and the continual nerve-wracking pop-pop-pop as we shot blindly into the darkness. I could see the flash from their weapons and when I saw one, I'd fire right back in the same direction. All we could do was hope that we got "them" before they got us. Fortunately, the shooting eventually stopped and it sounded as though the rivals were leaving. I sneaked back in through the rear door of the restaurant to scope out the situation. Seeing no one to fear, I then raced outside to our car, hopped in, and blasted down the alley where Joe was waiting. He jumped in and we roared away safely. Our other meeting buddies also took off, gravel flying.

A couple of days later, Joe and I went to Ben's Cafe Society for lunch. After we ordered our meal, Joe said, "You know, Chris, I'm really impressed with how well you held it together the other day during that shoot-out. You were just as cool as a cucumber. And that's exactly how you need to be to stay alive in a situation like that."

"Well, I feel lucky to be alive, Joe. That was pretty terrifying and I was worried that one of those bullets might find its way to you."

"Yeah, but one of them could have taken *you* out, too," he replied with a wry smile. "Everybody's at risk when it comes to bullets flying like that."

Our server brought the food to us just then. I nodded in agreement with Joe's comment, and we talked about business matters while enjoying our lunch. Naturally, I'd already received the customary "thank you" envelope stuffed with cash in thanks for my protection, and it felt good to know that my efforts weren't just taken for granted as part of the job I was hired to do.

Generally, when the bosses met, either with each other or with visiting cohorts, soldiers such as myself were usually stationed outside the doors, with orders to shoot immediately. That covered a lot of territory. Loyalty was essential; if someone wasn't trusted, that was it. Security was very tight, and expectations were high. It didn't matter whether we were in a public place like the Blue Gardenia, or in a more secluded spot in an office tucked away in a warehouse. I was always on guard and as watchful as a hawk.

One time Joe, Frank, and Stan were all together at a meeting at Skinny's. I was standing behind Joe and he told me to keep alert and to watch for people coming in the back door. As I was watching that back door, I heard the front door open and two men walked in. Instantly I knew we were going to have trouble, because they were from a rival team and wanted more territory for their racketeering business.

Joe stood up and made a friendly gesture to those two men and they all shook hands and sat down at the big table. It was clear they didn't like each other very much, and there was a lot of tension in the room. I was on high alert. Soon, Joe pushed back his chair and said, "This is what's going to happen. Your side will take a few more spots on the East side of town, including some we presently control, and in turn we will take some of yours on the West side. But no more meetings, and no more running into each other in these spots-- or you'll have a war on your hands."

To my relief, some kind of accord had been reached and the meeting ended quietly.

# # #

Paying scrupulous attention to detail applied to everything, even cash spent during "go-fer" errands. If I or any of the other lower echelon helpers was given money with which to make a purchase, he was expected to bring back *all* of the change, right down to the penny. I was very careful to always make sure that I could state the cost of a purchase, show the receipt, and hand over any change I'd received. Neither Joe nor Stan ever had to ask me about this, because I had it ready for them before they even thought of it. Or, at least, that's how it appeared to me. I'm sure I was being tested all the time for signs of skimming or other signs of misplaced loyalty, and I never, ever gave them cause to doubt me for a minute.

The first time I noticed this and was put to the test was when I was picking up a produce order from the guys. It was pushing noon and Joe said, "Hey, Chris, you got time to eat with us?"

I'd noticed those Italians really loved to eat, and usually favored the best they could get.

I looked at my watch. "Sure, Joe. Where do you want to go? Amico's? Skinny's?"

"Nah, the guys just want sandwiches to eat here. Tell you what, Chris," Joe said, pulling cash out of his pocket and tossing me a couple of twenties. "You know where the Bay & Goodwin Deli is?"

"Sure do," I replied.

Joe was scribbling something on a scratch pad.

"Take this list and the cash and run over there, would you? Give Mario the list and he'll make up the order. He knows what we like. That money should cover it okay."

I went over to that deli, and left it with a big bagful of goodies: Salami, roast beef, smoked turkey, corned beef, big loaves of fresh Italian bread, and several kinds of sliced cheese. And, not to forget, a jar of good mustard. The cash Joe'd given me covered the cost with a little left over, and I duly handed him his change--right down to the penny--when I returned to the Market.

"Thanks, Chris. Okay, everybody--dig in!"

Joe had spread some clean newspapers across a couple of lettuce crates at the back of the stall. He set out the bread, cold cuts, cheese, and mustard. Someone at the stall always had a knife, and one was appropriated for the mustard. By now, Mustache had wandered over and grinned in delight when he saw the spread. Papa Camp tore apart the first loaf of bread, piled an assortment of the sliced meats and cheeses on a chunk of it, slathered some mustard over that filling, and then clapped another chunk of bread on top. *"Mangiamo!"* (let's eat). He demonstrated by biting heartily into the sandwich.

I waited until the others had made their sandwiches, then helped myself, following their examples as I put mine together. That was the most delicious lunch I'd ever had. It was totally impromptu but the ingredients were top-notch, and I still remember, to this day, how savory those sandwiches really were. I've never been able to quite duplicate that taste. I guess the atmosphere had something to do with enhancing the flavor. That was my first time for those tasty sandwiches and it wasn't the last; every couple of weeks or so Joe would send me out for "all the fixin's" as he called it. I memorized the list of items and always brought back the change, no matter how many times I went on that errand.

Of course, Mario at the deli knew what Joe wanted and he would wordlessly start putting up the order as soon as I walked in the door. He never shortchanged Joe that I could see; of course, he knew better than to do that!

Returning the exact change to Joe as I'd done on that day also applied to the collections and shakedowns wherein I was assigned to visit businesses that owed protection money and hadn't paid it on time. Every penny had to be paid--and then some. You'll read about this in another chapter. I quickly found how powerful it felt to have a couple of big, beefy, strong-arm henchmen at the ready. One nod from me and they'd break a guy's arms or beat the crap out of him. Their very presence got the message across to the business owner. None of them was foolish enough to risk that; they paid up, pronto. The way I handled myself and learned so quickly meant that I had definitely "made my bones" in a way with the Organization and was making positive contributions to its operation.

Every day, I was running on sheer adrenaline. Getting very little sleep and being on call every minute was taking a toll on my body and mind. My family life was in a shambles, too, and I felt helpless; everything was out of control. But the money was too good and I wasn't ready to give it up—yet.

CHAPTER ELEVEN

Spring was in the air; it was warm enough to leave our topcoats behind.

"Chris," said Joe one morning, "We are going to need to go out of town over the weekend of May 10-13. I hope that will work for you, because I really need you to come with me."

Since that date was nearly a month away, I told him it would be no problem. Joe didn't explain or elaborate, but a few days prior to the tenth of May, he told me that we would be flying to Chicago for an important meeting. "Now, you just plan to wear a nice pair of slacks from your tailored wardrobe, a long-sleeved dress shirt, and one of your lighter leather jackets. Don't worry about bringing any personal effects. You'll have shaving stuff, toothbrush, and all of that waiting for you at the hotel."

Hmm. That was interesting. My Mob wardrobe included many choices so it wasn't hard to select something along those lines. Of course, none of the tailor-made clothing pieces had labels in them; that was to make tracing them to anyone—stores or individuals--pretty impossible.

"Do you want me to be packing?" Joe knew I was referring to carrying one or more guns.

"No, and I'm glad you checked with me first. Be sure to leave them in their usual storage spots." That meant they'd be left in the building Main Street where our wardrobes and other stuff was kept. I wondered why a man as cautious as Joe would leave his most important protection behind, but I would soon learn the answer.

On the appointed afternoon, we were driven to the Rochester airport by one of my colleague drivers. When we arrived in Chicago and got off the plane, we saw a uniformed chauffeur holding a discreet sign that read, "Joe and Chris." He drove us to a fancy hotel right in downtown Chicago. It was late evening by that time, and we went downstairs to its best restaurant for dinner.

Joe was nervous, and muttered, "I should have ordered what I needed for tonight instead of tomorrow," and we ate quickly. I was at the top of my game in being watchful, and the meal was concluded without incident.

We returned upstairs to our rooms, which were adjacent and connected by an inner door so that we could talk together privately, yet sleep separately.

To my surprise, our clothing and personal effects were hung up in the closets or placed in the bathrooms as appropriate. I saw my best evening tuxedo was there, along with the requisite frilled shirt, bow tie, cummerbund, and polished black shoes. Some casual street-type clothing was also neatly hung and unwrinkled, as fresh as if it had just been dry cleaned an hour earlier. Socks and underwear had been included, too. Shaving gear, toothpaste, and a packaged toothbrush and other toiletries occupied the bathroom vanity. I was all set!

I tried to sleep as much as possible, but something about Joe's demeanor had made me nervous. So, it was a relief when he knocked at our connecting door and called me into his room early the next morning.

Suddenly, there was a knock at the main room door. I looked at Joe, and he murmured, "Look first, and then open it. I'm expecting breakfast."

So, I looked through the peephole and saw what appeared to be a hotel employee like a bellhop with a room-service cart. Carefully, I opened the door partway. Joe was standing right behind me, and said, "Yes, come right in, please."

On the top shelf of the cart was a very large silver platter, covered by a well-polished silver dome. It looked to me like something out of the movies, and I thought, "Ooh, an elegant breakfast! Way to go, Joe!"

As the bellboy started to back the car from the room, Joe made a motion with his head. I quickly pulled a $50 bill from my pocket and gave it to the employee. After he left, I closed and locked the door.

Joe said, "I'm hungry. Let's go get something to eat."

I stared at him in confusion. "But, isn't that our breakfast in there?" I asked, pointing to the dome-covered platter. My mouth was already anticipating something elegant and tasty.

Joe laughed, and said, "Lift up that cover, Chris." I did, and to my total shock, there lay two semiautomatic .45s, gleaming in the light. "See, you funny North Country boy," Joe joked, "Things aren't always what they seem. Come on, let's go."

We slid the guns into our respective shoulder holsters, put on our jackets, and headed out to find some real breakfast. The hotel bellhop captain had recommended a busy café a short distance away. We walked down a couple of blocks and found the place. It had a full delicatessen counter as well as booths and tables. Before long, we were wrapping ourselves around plates of sausages, eggs, and toast, as well as some excellent coffee.

As we stood to leave, Joe murmured, "Let's find a payphone. I need to make a couple of calls."

In those days before everyone carried cellular telephones, it was easy to find a phone booth. I stood right beside it while Joe made some calls. Then we went for a walk.

A bit apprehensive as always, Joe asked, "Anyone following us?"

I shook my head; I'd already made sure we didn't have a tail. Eventually, we came to a large cigar store and went in. To the left, in a small alcove in the back was a pay phone

"There we go!" Joe exclaimed. "Chris, pick out some cigars for us; you know what I like." He went to that phone and made some more calls.

As we left the cigar store, Joe mentioned, "There'll be a Lincoln limo coming to pick us up. We're going to meet some people I know. They have information I'll need for tonight. From now on, until we get back to the hotel this evening, no talking. Just be observant and aware as you always are of what's going on around us."

With those somewhat terse instructions, I buttoned my lip accordingly and didn't say another word.

Joe and I walked to a particular street corner, and saw that waiting limo and got in. The driver took us to a railroad station, where we got out and I followed Joe around it to a separate building, set back from the tracks. We went in and saw three or four Italian guys in there, all smoking cigars in the tiny room. Joe shook hands with each of them and they all sat down a big table that dwarfed the room. I stood directly behind Joe like an invisible man; no one said anything to me.

One of the men handed Joe a flat package. I watched Joe remove four large photographs, two each of two different individuals. Joe looked at them closely, then put them together with some paperwork from the package, after looking it over, too.

I could see that one of the photos was of a man, all dressed up in a white tux at some kind of fancy function, probably a wedding. A second photo of him was a plain mug shot, sans fancy clothing. The other two photos were of another man, one apparently from the same function, as he also wore a white tux. A mug shot of him was similar to the first guy—plain, bare-bones, black-and-white.

Indicating the second man's photo, Joe murmured to me, sotto voce, "This is the guy you'll be watching tonight. Never take your eyes off him, and watch his eye. Any move he makes, you be ready to shoot."

I nodded.

Then all of the men began talking, mostly in Italian, which I don't speak and can't understand. Sometimes the voices were raised and the hand gestures told me that the discussion wasn't all positive.

Finally, they all stood up. Joe shook hand all around and we went outside to the Lincoln limo, which was still waiting.

As we rode through the streets, Joe looked at his watch and said, "It's time for pizza; I hear that this place is good."

The driver pulled up in front of a pizza joint. Joe got out, leaving the packet with the photos and paperwork sitting on the car seat. I poked Joe and pointed to it; Joe just shook his head. "Come on."

As we walked in the door, an older Italian gentleman greeted us and spoke to Joe in his language. They shook hands and he led us to a back table. Joe ordered wine and I had a soft drink. Soon, the man brought us a big tray bearing slices of two or three different kinds of pizza. It was excellent. Joe loved good food, and he didn't stint on how much he ate.

The owner also brought us a plate of cannoli, Joe's favorite dessert. They were very tasty. Coming over to remove our plates, the man chatted with us; it was just mundane conversation. While this was going on, another man had entered the restaurant, carrying a briefcase. He walked over, set it down beside the owner, and left. The owner picked it up and set it down on the table in front of Joe.

He spoke just four words, in English. "You'll find that sufficient."

Following Joe's lead, I stood up and we started for the door. Joe always had me go first to check things out. I'd thought that was pretty cool at first, until it penetrated my thick skull that it meant if lead was flying, it would hit me first.

Anyway, we got back in the waiting limo. Joe put the briefcase on his knees and popped the latches. It was full to the brim with banded bundles of U.S. currency. Joe picked up that brown packet containing the photos and papers, laid it on top of the cash, and fastened the briefcase shut. He set it down on the floor as casually as could be.

It was mid-afternoon, and Joe instructed the driver to take us on a scenic tour of the city. We drove along the famous lakeshore drive and gazed out the windows at various landmarks. Finally, Joe said it was time to return to the hotel, and we pulled up in front of it and got out.

As we entered the lobby, Joe said that he wanted to rest for a while. "We have to be on top of our game tonight, Chris."

Back in our adjoining guest rooms, we removed our jackets and shoulder holsters. Joe handed me the packet and instructed me to memorize the men's faces. There could be no mistaken identities; we must be sure that the men we would see later were those depicted in the photographs.

The "principal," as I'd call him, was a man probably in his early sixties, a bit older than Joe. The other individual, his bodyguard, was taller than me, and even thinner. His height made me a bit nervous; he was also older, likely in his early forties. I studied their faces until I thought I'd be able to pick them out in a crowd anywhere.

"Good," Joe nodded. "We're going to the opera tonight. Have you ever been before?"

"Nope," I replied. A North Country boy like me was pretty much a country western fan.

Joe chuckled. "It's probably just as well; I don't want you getting interested in what's happening on stage. You'll need to be paying attention to other things."

He went on to explain that we would be accompanied by female escorts who would be waiting for us downstairs in the lobby. "We'll have box seats in the balcony, and these two guys in the photos are going to be there, too. Your job will be to protect me. If that bodyguard blinks twice, just blow him away."

"Got it," I replied.

After we'd each had a shower in our respective bathrooms, Joe and I got dressed in our evening tuxedos. We put on our shoulder holsters, tucked in the guns, and put on the formal jackets. Boy, did we look classy, right down to our white *boutonnieres*, which were waiting for us in our rooms when we arrived back from the afternoon's activities.

As we got downstairs to the big main lobby, Joe gestured over to a corner. "There they are," he said quietly. Two very attractive women rose from their chairs as we approached them. They were beautifully gowned and wore elaborate corsages.

The four of us went out to a waiting limousine, and chatted together during the drive to the opera venue. An usher showed us to our seats, and as we neared them, another group of people entered from an opposite door. It was our expected quarry, also accompanied by two lovely gals. As they came towards us, my eyes were on the designated bodyguard and his face definitely matched the one in the photograph.

Joe and the other principal took their seats, while I stood right behind him, as the other guy's bodyguard assumed his stance directly behind his boss. The two men leaned in close to each other, talking intensely. Then Joe gave a sign, raising his hand up towards the other bodyguard. His boss nodded his head and Joe slowly and carefully removed that brown packet from his jacket pocket and slid it over to the other boss. I suspected that it must contain the papers included with the photographs, and it turned out I was right. The other man didn't bother to check it, just tucked it into an inside pocket of his jacket.

At intermission, we all got up to leave, each party going our separate ways to exit the balcony. Outside, the limousine was waiting, as usual, and we returned to the hotel. I never saw either of those men again, and although I've tried to piece it together, I still don't know who they were.

Our female escorts went their own way as we walked into the lobby. Joe and I headed back to our rooms for some rest; we had an early morning return flight to Rochester.

Joe told me to get those pictures that lay on my dressers in my hotel room. He popped open that briefcase and tucked them on top of the cash.

I just had to ask, "Joe, how did you dare to leave all that cash here in your room? Someone came in to leave those boutonnieres; they could have snooped and taken it."

"No way," Joe shook his head. "The bellhop and maid are both on our payroll. If anything came up missing, so would they, and they know it. They're our associates, in fact, just playing assigned roles."

Joe was visibly relaxed; he knew he could trust them all, as well as me. I'm still not sure, to this day, exactly what business had been transacted that day, but he was happy about it.

Over time, I had realized that many of the big-city pizzerias were just fronts for money-laundering schemes and movement of drugs and guns. That one we'd visited in Chicago was certainly quite a hub of Mob business. I could see that just from the hour or so we spent there.

We got up at 6:30 the next morning to catch our return flight. Joe carried that briefcase everywhere with him—even to the public bathrooms. I was always right there with him, standing guard.

Back at the Rochester airport, a limo picked us up and took us to the Market. It was closed that Sunday as usual, but A.J., brother Louie, and Papa Camp were all waiting for us in the business office. Joe immediately kissed Papa and assured the others that all had gone very well. He set the briefcase up on his desk, and opened it. Then Joe pulled out one of the bundles of currency and flipped through the bills. A.J. and Louie did the same. I stood there as a silent observer, watching them grinning over their spoils. Papa Camp smiled at all of them and then said, in his heavily-accented English, "Time to go home."

We all got ready to leave. His sons would drive him home that day.

"See you tomorrow," Joe told me. "By the way, Chris, you can keep those clothes you're wearing."

He referred to the tailored trousers, shirt, and leather jacket I'd worn for the flights back and forth from Chicago.

"Hey—thanks!" Usually all of my mob clothing had to stay in the wardrobe over on Main Street. This was a nice little bonus-- good clothes that I didn't have to pay for.

My personal car was parked in the Family's garage. I got it out and drove over to the building on Main Street and went upstairs where I'd left my street clothes on Friday. I changed into them, and carefully folded the gift clothing to take home.

When I got there, I showed the clothes to Norma, saying just that they were a little present from the boss. "I'm sorry that I had to be gone these last couple of days, but I had no choice."

I didn't elaborate and Norma didn't ask any questions. I'm not sure now how much she knew then, but she probably suspected that I was into the Mob pretty deep. And she was into her own brand of deceit, big time. But, it was Sunday afternoon and time for us to at least go through the motions of doing some family stuff with our children. That becomes very difficult (and sad) when you know your marriage is going up in smoke.

CHAPTER TWELVE

Ah, yes, my personal life—what there was of it. Well, what there was of it was going to hell in a hand basket. I felt as though I was in a squirrel cage, running all the time in circles and powerless to stop it.

Since Italian families are known for closeness and loyalty, and dote on their children, both Joe and Stan were mindful and understanding of my home life situation. I appreciated that they did their best to accommodate me when some domestic matter needed my attention.

The situation at home began taking a turn for the very worst, as far as I was concerned. I'd already caught Norma in a very compromised situation with Barry Peterson, a neighborhood handyman who'd done some electrical work for us. That had sparked quite a shouting match, with Norma maintaining the viewpoint that I was "making something out of nothing."

My opinion was that she was making hay while the sun shone, so to speak--taking advantage of my absence to pursue her own extracurricular activities that were sexually based. As my daily work hours lengthened, it was often 7 p.m. or later by the time I arrived home, so I was disadvantaged to monitor what was happening on the home scene.

"Daddy, Daddy!" My three kids rushed me as I got out of the car one evening.

"Hey, there, you three—what's going on?" I laughed at their eager faces and boundless energy. To me, they were wonderful little beings and I regretted not being home to spend more time with them.

Roseanne, the eldest, spoke up importantly. "Uncle Mike was here today. He brought us candy and a new card game."

"Oh, he did? That's nice."

While I smiled reassuringly, my mind was clicking like a telegraph line. "Uncle Mike" was my stepbrother, and he seemed to be visiting our home several times a month—usually while I wasn't at home. Of course, he had lived with us, on and off, for a few months after he and Julie had divorced and he was busy with his job at Xerox and finding a new place to live. But he'd finally found an apartment in the area, moved in, and established a new life for himself during the previous year. I could understand an occasional drop-in visit, but not during the weekdays and especially, when I wasn't home. After all, he was MY stepbrother—not Norma's.

The kids and I went into the house. Norma came forward to kiss me as usual. She smiled and I tried to put my suspicions out of my mind. "Anything happening?" I asked casually.

"No, not much. I made some doughnuts today and picked up those new curtains from Robbins Department Store. Don't they look nice?" Norma gestured towards the kitchen windows.

Dutifully, I glanced over and nodded, "Yeah. Nice." My eyes strayed to the center of the kitchen table and I saw a bowl of wrapped candies. As I walked to the refrigerator and took out a beer, I saw a boxed card game sat on the counter nearby. I picked it up.

Norma had been watching me, and now she chuckled and said, "I bought that for the kids while I was out, and got them some candy."

I looked straight at her and wondered why she was lying. "Why was Mike here today?"

My wife turned away and pretended to be busy taking a dish from the cupboard. "He wasn't here. What makes you say that?"

"Because Roseanne said he stopped by and brought the candy and cards. But you said you bought them. Which is the truth?"

"Oh, Honey, you know how Roseanne likes to pretend! She really likes her Uncle Mike and daydreams about things. She always wants people to bring her presents. Making up stories is perfectly normal for her. I guess she just has trouble separating real life from daydreams.

"Here," said Norma, pouring milk and setting food on the table. "Dinner's ready."

I didn't want to get into it with Norma over dinner. The kids were all chattering about school and play matters and it was family time, such as it was. But I thought plenty.

The next day, at the market, Joe asked me how things were going at home. I shook my head.

"Something's going on. My stepbrother seems to be stopping by a lot, always when I'm not there. Roseanne, my daughter—she's eight—told me he'd been by and brought them candy and a game. But Norma swore that he hadn't been there at all. Things don't feel right, but I can't quite put my finger on what's wrong."

"Do you think she's cheating on you?"

I shrugged. "Dunno. She's always hotter than a pistol when it's bedtime. But I did notice some fancy new underwear in the laundry basket and I've never seen it on her. That makes me wonder. And, my stepbrother, Mike, still seems to be hanging out a lot at our house—when I'm not there. And there've been a couple of incidents that I'm not sure about."

"Hmm. Would you like me to have someone check a few times a week, make a note of any visitors?"

"Wow, you'd do that for me?" Joe's suggestion was the answer to my unspoken wish.

"Sure. I've got guys checking out some stuff over that way all the time. They can buzz by and write down license plate numbers and stuff."

"Thanks, Joe." I shook his hand.

It seemed as though the subject of sex was going to stay with me even at work, because the next subject Joe discussed was a plan involving making pornographic videos.

"Our guys and friends work hard, and we want to give them a little fun that goes beyond dinner and dancing," Joe told me. "That includes you. I want you to drive me over there; it'll be in Rochester at one of the hotels. Make sure you have time on the twelfth; that's on a Tuesday." He winked at me. "Right now, I need to go to a lunch meeting over at the Blue Gardenia with Stan, Frank, Sammy G, and Rene. Let's take the black Lincoln Limo; you can drive us over there. A.J.'s coming along, too."

The lunch meeting went off without incident, although A.J., as usual, was bad-tempered and tried to argue with Stan, mostly in Italian. Since I always tuned them out and just concentrated on voice volume and body language, I have no idea what was being discussed. It seemed to end in some kind of accord, though, and we drove back to the parking/storage garage without incident.

"I'm taking Joe to a big meeting today," I told Norma as I left for work the on the twelfth of Tuesday. "I don't think I'll be too late, but I can't say for sure."

"Okay, Honey," Norma smiled. "Maybe we can have a snack together when you get home. I'll be waiting up for you."

That "snack" she referred to was our euphemism for having sex. And, it seemed to me that Norma was already doing her share of "snacking" with other people—or, at least, that's what I strongly suspected. As I drove towards the city, I mulled over what Joe had told me a few days earlier, over a private lunch.

"Chris, my boys have been checking out your place during the past week couple of weeks, like we talked about."

He consulted a slip of paper. "Anyone you know drive a blue Buick Special?" Joe rattled off a license number.

"Yeah, my stepbrother, Mike. Anyone else?"

"Ah, a tan Chevy Impala." Again, Joe enumerated a license number.

Damn, I thought. That car belonged to my best friend, Hank. "Yes, that's my buddy Hank's car."

"Some buddy," Joe commented wryly. "He's been there at least four times since the boys have been checking. The Buick's been there twice this past week. I actually had the guys stake out the house and see how long those cars have been there each time. They timed 'em. It was always for at least an hour," Joe said, shaking his head. "And sometimes, the cars were still there when your kids got home from school."

"I can't thank you enough, Joe. I'll take it from here." I shook his hand.

"You know, Chris, we can take care of things, if you want us to," Joe mentioned. "We can 'persuade' her to behave herself, or take it further than that—whatever you want."

It was clear what he was offering and a chill ran down my spine. My wife might be cheating on me, but she was the mother of my children. Taking her out of the gene pool—or even just slapping her around—wasn't the answer. Of course, years later, I questioned myself about the wisdom of that decision, but one can't undo what's been done or go back and change history.

That night, I cut right to the chase with Norma. "Are you fucking around on me?" I looked her right in the eye.

"Why do you say that? No way!"

Her face didn't give away anything, although she looked down.

"I noticed you've been having a lot of male company when I'm not here. Mike, Hank, others . . ." I let my voice trail off.

"Oh, for Pete's sake, Chris. They always hope they'll catch you here--they just want to see *you*. They want to know how everything's going, no big deal. And they like to see the kids."

As she continued speaking, Norma seemed angry and became indignant at being accused of unfaithful. "Who are you to be accusing *me*?" She shrilled at me. "I have no idea of what you're doing all day and half the night in Rochester. How dare you?"

To get by these issues, within minutes, Norma couldn't wait to get her panties off and have sex with me. With hindsight, I know now that I was the King of gullible idiots. But wanting to think the best of my wife was a lot less painful than confronting her infidelity. Like a fool, I let it slide—until the next time, which came sooner than I expected.

I guess Joe decided to try to put the wind up Norma, because a few nights later, we were sitting in the living room and suddenly heard gunfire close by. I peeked out and saw someone in a dark car aiming a rifle just above house and there was another loud report. Norma shrieked as I motioned her to get down, and then the car pulled away.

"You dumb ass!" I shouted at her. "You know who that was? That's why I warned you to stop fucking around! That kind of two-timing behavior isn't tolerated in some circles. They're warning you and you'd better pay attention!"

"What do you mean? How do you know who it was?" Norma was scared and upset.

"The folks I work for don't play games, Norma. They've been keeping an eye on you; that's how I found out about your afternoon 'visitors' and what you've been doing. Let's put it this way: they don't approve. You keep this up, you might not live to tell about it."

Norma's fear morphed into irritation and anger. "What I do is nobody's business. I'm not hurting anybody." She looked me straight in the face. "I just like to fuck--that's what I like to do. And if you're not around and aren't man enough to take care of me, well, what do you expect me to do?"

She stormed out of the room and came back through in her coat and scarf. "I'm going to the store for milk and bread!" And she was gone. She returned in about an hour and neither of us spoke to each other for the rest of the night. I had plenty of time to not get any sleep.

CHAPTER THIRTEEN

That red-letter day, Tuesday, the twelfth, was upon us. I drove Joe and A.J. to a popular Rochester hotel. We went upstairs to a large suite of rooms with two large King beds in the first room, and through the open archway to the next room, I saw several dining tables with chairs all on one side, facing into the other room. A bar was set up along one wall. To my shock, two lovely young women and two good-looking men—all stark naked—were talking to another man.

"Come on, let's sit down," Joe suggested, leading the way into the dining room. Damn, I hated taking my eyes off those gals! As I sat down at the table, I realized it had been deliberately positioned to give us all a ringside view of those big beds in the next room. That's why there were only chairs on one side of the table.

We were all served drinks from the bar by other, very skimpily-dressed women. I noticed menu cards had been laid at each place. I picked up mine and started to read it.

Wow! This menu was unlike any I'd seen before. It was printed on nice paper, and from a distance, resembled a conventional restaurant menu. But, "Today's Specials" sure differed from customary fare! On the front was a photograph of a smiling, sexy woman in a very underdressed way, if you get my drift.

"Janice," it read. "Blonde, 28 years old, vital stats: 38-27-37, married."   Then, beneath that, was another name. "Darcy, brunette, 27 years old, vital stats: 36-25-36, married." These names were followed simply by two men's names: "Bob" and "Dave."

Below these names was a list of sexual acts being offered for viewing and what the "stars" were paid for each act. Good grief, I'd never seen anything like this before.

MENU
"Blow job, woman on man . . . $100
"Regular intercourse". . . $200
"Hand job". . . $100
"Anal sex". . . $300
"Three-way" . . . $450
"Two women" . . . $350

"Combinations" . . . $600+
"Play with sex toys" . . . 200

At the bottom of this menu was a notation that viewers could "order" any of these items as a kind of dessert, to participate in and enjoy privately following the show of these acts which were all going to be done now right in front of us.

I'm sure my eyes were as big as saucers and I truly felt like a country bumpkin at that moment. This was beyond anything I'd ever even fantasized about in my wildest dreams.

"See those guys with the cameras?" Joe told us. "They'll be filming everything you see here today. We ship a lot of these movies overseas; there's a big market here and we get more money for them there than within this country. The men over there just eat it up—practically inhale the sight of those American women getting fucked."

So, I was going to watch a porno movie live, as it was being filmed! Those women were something else. I found out later that one of them was married to a Kodak employee, the other to someone at Xerox.

What a different way to make money, I thought, watching as Janice knelt beside the bed where Bob sat, waiting. She played with his dick for a moment until he had an obvious erection, and I salivated with each stroke of her tongue. You could almost feel it. Ouch! My wife wasn't bad at fellatio, but this gal could teach her a thing or two. Or, so I thought at the time. More on that later.

A few minutes later, rather than taking him to ejaculation, Janice slowly got up and laid back on the bed while Dave climbed on top of her. He rammed his sizable dick into her and began socking it to her, very hard. A few minutes later she writhed and moaned as though she had reached orgasm. Dave pulled out of Janice (he still hadn't come) and then Darcy replaced him. He and Bob sat on the other bed and watched as she and Janice went into a lengthy woman-woman coupling.

I never saw so much different positioning and rolling around, and it was my first time seeing two women giving each other oral sex. They were quite a pair. And yet, they were both married--to men. That blew my mind; they were so expert at what they were doing and appeared to be enjoying it. Of course, that was just an act, literally. But their pretense of having fun was very convincing.

Various episodes followed, with the women using a big dildo on each other, two men working on one woman at a time, two women servicing one man, and so on. Finally, for a finale, both men went back on top of the women for conventional sex and each pulled out at the last minute and ejaculated on the women's breasts. They had managed to keep going without coming for all that time. I'm sure they'd taken some kind of drug to keep it up for that long. Viagra and Cialis weren't readily available to the average guy then, but the porn industry apparently had something that worked.

After that finale, I was kind of overdone and feeling extremely horny, of course.

Joe leaned over towards me. "Want to stay and have some fun, Chris? I can get a ride back to the office."

It was awfully tempting, but I resisted and shook my head. "No, I've got stuff to get done this afternoon. Thanks anyway, Joe."

That took a lot of will power on my part—or, was it "won't" power?

We left and I dropped Joe off at the Market, then called on customers for the rest of the afternoon.

That night, I started describing for Norma the day's entertainment. Her eyes got big and excited.

"Those women make so much money for what they do," I said, after explaining about all the different sex acts that had taken place. "It's amazing."

The more I talked about it, the hotter Norma got. I, too, was pretty aroused after everything I'd actually seen and then described. It was to be some time before I'd find that Norma already knew all about the making of those porn videos.

"Did you have to pay to watch?" Norma asked, quickly unbuttoning her blouse. "How many of you guys were there?" She was down to her panties in record time.

"No, Joe paid about $100 for each of us to be there. It was a thank-you for us, a little break in the routine. There were eight or nine guys in our group, maybe 25 fellas in all."

"Boy, I wish I'd been there!" Norma had completely stripped and was frantically unzipping my slacks. Already wet, she couldn't wait for me to be inside her. I was just as ready as she was. What a way to go, I thought, fully enjoying myself and conveniently not thinking, for an hour or so, about my cheating wife and how my marriage was in ruins.

What Norma hadn't said, after hearing about that little porno party, was that she wished she'd been one of the players. She loved to show off her body and I'm sure she'd have fucked every guy in that room if given the chance.

Why was sex running--and ruining--my life?

I should have known better, but my middle name back then was "Naive." Once she found out that kind of money could be made in exchange for sex, the horse was out of the barn as far as Norma was concerned. I found that out as time passed.   If I hadn't put her up on such a sentimental pedestal--the love of my life, the mother of my children, the perfect lover--maybe the clouds around my head would have cleared. Unfortunately, many lies and betrayals still stood between me and that horrible day of enlightenment which awaited me down the road.

CHAPTER FOURTEEN

I met Joe in his office as prearranged. "You said you wanted to do some collections. Got anyone in mind?" he queried.

"Yeah," I replied. "The guy who owns that place across from the airport—Marvin Whatshisface. You know where I mean?"

Joe looked grim. "I sure do. Marvin owes money to quite a few people. He's a real jerk. How much is he into your company for?"

"Oh, around $400," I told him. "He's been running behind for months. Enough that it's time he coughed it up." (Remember, this was in the late 1960's, when $400 was a lot more money than it sounds like today.)

Joe nodded. "You go see Stan and explain the situation to him. He'll get you what you need."

In Stan Valenti's office, I repeated my conversation with Joe. He listened carefully, looking directly at me. Then he leaned forward.

"Okay, Chris," Stan said, looking me right in the eye, "I don't like that guy anyway, he's a dirty little crook. Here's what's gonna happen. You plan to be there at the restaurant tonight, a little after 11:30. I'll have a couple of our guys meet you, but they'll park around the rear of the building and stay by the back door. Remember, you won't have to get your hands dirty; they'll do the bull work. You'll be calling the plays, and they'll do whatever you tell 'em. Let me know tomorrow morning about how it went, okay?"

As I left Stan's office, my mind was racing; this was going to be a first for me, a situation where I'd be in charge and could really have some power as a Mob associate.

By the time I'd made all of my usual deliveries for the afternoon, it was quite late. It didn't make sense to drive all the way home, only to turn around in an hour or so and drive back to the city. So, I called Norma and told her I wouldn't be home until some time after midnight. Then I went back to the building where we had our wardrobes, changed into my regular street clothes, and went out to get some dinner. I ran into a couple of other produce business guys and shot the bull with them to pass the time.

At 11:40 p.m., I pulled into the parking lot of the restaurant across from the airport. A couple of minutes later, a dark sedan pulled in and I watched as it went around behind the building. I waited for a couple of more minutes, and then got out and went in the front door, which led directly into the bar. Fred, the regular bartender, was doing evening cleanup, and there were just one or two customers. They were getting ready to leave, and I waited until they had gone. Then I told Fred it was time for him to go home.

"Hey!" Fred objected, a scowl spreading across his face. "What the hell is going on? You don't tell me what to do, you little--"

I leaned back a bit and let my jacket fall open. The gleaming .45 tucked into my waistband was fully in view. "Oh, yes, I do. If you know what's good for you, you'll get out that door as fast as your legs can carry you. And keep your mouth shut. You call the police, you're dead meat. Go--now!"

Fred's eyes got real big. He quickly stepped over to a wall cupboard, grabbed a jacket off the hook, and he was out the door. I walked over and locked it.

Then I went into the kitchen, where I knew Marvin would be counting the day's cash. Sure enough, there he was, and at first he started to protest but saw my gun at the same instant. Still, the fat pig actually jumped up from his chair and tried to escape out the back door. I stood there grinning as he yanked it open and found two burly henchmen waiting. They pushed him back into the kitchen and then each took one of his arms and lifted him off the floor.

In a way, it was really funny to see--this slob of a guy still in his greasy, stained apron, his legs dangling and kicking as he struggled to regain his footing. The burly guys holding him grinned, too.

But Marvin wasn't smiling.

"What the hell's going on?" He demanded to know. The color was draining from his face and I saw sweat coming out all over him.

"There's a little matter of how much you owe my employer," I told him. "And, you're going to pay every cent of it, right now." I stuck the invoice in his face.

Marvin's eyes bulged. "Geez, I can't do that, it will leave me short for tomorrow and—"

"Too bad, you should have thought of that before you ran up such a bill. Now, get the money together. You see this invoice amount? I know there's that much cash just laying on the counter there."

Marvin glanced again at the bill. "Yeah, yeah, okay, I can do that. Put me down so I can count it out."

I nodded to the guys, and they simply dropped Marvin. He hit the floor hard, stumbled and got to his feet, then quickly moved over to the table where the cash lay. The invoice was for something over $400, so he counted out that amount and handed it to me.

"Nope." I shook my head. "There's interest involved, you know, more than what's here on the counter. You'd better go empty the bar till. I'll go with you."

Marvin protested, "You can't do that! I'm paying what I owe!"

I nodded to the henchmen and they moved forward. I also pulled the .45 from my waistband.

"No! I'll get it!"

Marvin hurried to the swinging door and I followed him out to the cash register in the bar.

"All of it," I told him, holding the gun steady in my hand.

I could see that he was freaking out, and it was tremendously amusing and exhilarating to me that I had this guy right where I wanted him. I was acutely aware of my personal power just then, and it was a real adrenaline rush. Confidently, I tucked the gun back into my waistband, knowing the henchmen were close by.

We returned to the kitchen, where Marvin counted up the remaining cash there and added the bar's takings. After clearing my company's invoice, there was some $800 left over. I picked up all of it.

"Fine," I said. "Now your bill's paid in full."

"You can't do this! I'm going to call the police!" Marvin shouted. Again, I reached for the .45.

His eyes widened again. "No, no, forget it!"

"That's right, and you damned well better pay your bills on time from now on. And if you decide to call anyone or tell anyone about this, it'll be the last time you say anything. *Because you're being watched--all the time*. If we have to come back, you'll leave this place in a bloody body bag, believe me," I told Marvin.

To drive the point home, the henchmen again took a menacing step forward.

"Okay, just go. Leave me alone! I won't do anything."

"Now you're learning," I told him. "You're seeing to reason."

I thumped him on the chest. "Remember to pay your bills on time and there won't be further trouble."

I gave a nod to the henchmen and they went out the back door. Marvin walked quietly with me to the front entry and I heard him deadbolt the door after I left.

The next day, I went to Stan's office, and spread the $800 on the counter. "Here's the extra money I got, Stan," I told him. "Marvin cleared the company's invoice but I told him he owed interest. I hope that was all right."

Stan laughed. "Say, you're catching on just fine, Chris! Good job, I like the way you think."

He made no move to take the money so I thought I should just leave. I started for the door.

"Hey, you're forgetting something! Here." Stan gestured to the cash.

"Mine?" I asked, surprised that he would give it all to me.

"Yeah, you earned it with your smart thinking. Take it and enjoy it." Stan dismissed me with a wave of his hand and turned away.

He didn't have to tell me twice; I pocketed the bills and left the office, floating on air. When I got home that evening, I stashed about $300 of the cash for myself, and gave the remaining $500 to my wife.

"Here," I said, "Put it into the household expense fund."

Her eyed widened, then I saw the greed in them as she slid the bills into her purse. But it didn't faze me just then. I was so thrilled with what had gone down that night and making all of that extra money was just fantastic. Greed was everywhere, I reckoned-- so what? Everybody likes money.

That first solo shakedown I performed opened the door and my eyes to the
widespread extortion and racketeering that was the bread and butter for the Rochester Family. Joe and Stan started sending me and another flunky, Vince (we called him Vinnie), out to do collections at quite a few small, mom-and-pop businesses. Most of them were run by foreign-born people, mostly Asians and Middle Easterners.

We would walk into the establishment, such as a convenience store or dry cleaners, and the owner would silently place an envelope on the counter. I knew what was in there and just as silently nodded and slid the envelope into my jacket pocket. These already-struggling business owners were paying for us to not shoot up the place, hurt their families, or otherwise make their lives miserable--or, worse yet, non-existent.

"What a way to make money!" Vinnie exulted. He was quite high on the ready cash, pussy, and other perks of working for the Mob, and showed no remorse for what we were doing. My conscience nagged at me a bit, but I, too, was way too thrilled by the money and power to let the exploitation of those business owners overwhelm me.

A few weeks later, I joined the boys, as I'd come to fondly think of them, at a special dinner gathering at a local restaurant for various produce business owners in the area. My boss, Sam Fields, from the company that officially employed me, had been included because Joe wanted to discuss a business proposition with him.

Sam was duly impressed with the expensive dinner and the booze flowing freely. Eventually, he'd had a little too much bourbon, and it nearly led to disaster. A.J. was talking to Sam about business and giving him some advice on a particular matter relating to produce ordering tricks.

Sam bristled up and I could see him starting to get belligerent. "Well, so you think you can tell me what to do and how to do it, you damned *Guinea Wop*?" Sam smirked at A.J.

I'd never seen someone's eyes literally blaze before, but the look of hatred and loathing A.J. gave Sam almost set the room on fire. In a heartbeat, A.J. had pulled out his .45 and moved towards Sam. Three more seconds and Sam would be toast.

Without thinking of my own safety, I quickly jumped between them. "Sam, you should keep your big, fat mouth shut! A.J., this guy's really just a dumb shit, don't pay attention to him. He's just an ignorant fool. Please, please put the gun away, you don't want to do this."

A.J. was seething. "Yes, I do!" He shouted. "Nobody calls me a *'Guinea Wop'* and lives to tell about it. I don't have to take that shit from anyone!"

Suddenly, in a swift move by A.J., I felt that .45 pressed against *my* temple, for the second time in my life. From focusing on Sam, A.J. was now glaring at me. His eyes were still blazing and I could literally feel the heat of his anger.

Shaking but determined, I tried to remain calm and soothe him. "You're right, A.J., you sure don't have to take that shit from him--or anyone. But violence isn't going to make Sam any smarter. I'll straighten him out--don't worry. Just put the gun away!"

This comes under the category of "what was I thinking?" I'd engaged in a lot of risky stuff in my life already, and now I was putting my life on the line to save another. My intentions were honorable and my action would be rewarded, but that's not what was on my mind just then. I just didn't want to see bloodshed and mayhem.

By that time, Joe had hurried over to us and hissed at A.J. "You damned fool--drop it!" He took A.J.'s gun away from him and I went into a bit of momentary aftershock. Jesus--I could have been killed! Then Joe pulled his brother away from me and Sam. They moved away into the next room and I knew that Joe was reaming A.J. out.

But A.J. wasn't through.

The next day, when I walked into the Camp's office, A.J. was waiting for me. He again pulled out his .45 and aimed it directly at me. The scowl on his face and his blazing eyes were enough to make a toad's blood run cold. Mine felt like ice water.

"Chris, don't you ever, ever do that again! You don't get between me and that jackass, you don't interfere with me and my business. I almost shot you, ya jerk! In fact, maybe I still should!"

I could hardly breathe and was trying to get my vocal cords to work when Joe suddenly came into the office, saw what was going on, and, once again, quickly intervened. He'd evidently heard at least the tail end of A.J.'s rant.

"Put that gun down, A.J.! You're the one who's the jackass here! I'm always telling you to control that temper of yours. You're going to get us into trouble—big trouble! Like I told you last night, the last thing we want is to call attention to ourselves, the business, people we work with. If you'd shot that damned fool Sam—or Chris--there'd have been hell to pay all around. Thank God Chris prevented a disaster. You ought to be grateful; I know I am!"

Joe was vehement now, glaring at A.J. I'd never seen him so fired up and angry. He thumped his brother on the chest for emphasis. "Keep your head and keep your temper—is that clear?"

Without saying a word, A.J. tucked the handgun back into his shoulder holster and picked up his suit jacket. He moved to the door.

"Yeah, right," he growled finally, with one last glare at both of us, and the door slammed behind him.

"Boy, Chris, that really was a foolhardy move on your part, you could have been killed last night. I admire your courage. But, that brother of mine is such a hothead. I'm sorry he threatened you just now, too." Joe shook his head ruefully. Well," he added, "I'm so thankful that you did intervene, because it prevented a real major incident from happening."

I sighed. "Joe, this is a case of the chickens coming home to roost. Sam has a history of several bad personality traits, you might say. First, he shoots his mouth off without thinking. Second, he drinks too much, and that leads to him flapping his lips even more. Third, he has a habit of calling people 'derogatory' names."

"Really? You mean like what happened last night with him calling A.J. a *Guinea Wop*?"

I nodded. "Exactly. That's one of his favorites. See, there are several Italian guys working in or associated with the produce company, including Stefano, Alfredo, and Guido. And dumb-assed Sam, well, it doesn't take much to fire him up, and when he gets pissed, he'll yell something like, 'Figure it out, ya goddam *Guinea Wop*!' to one of them.

"While that sounds--and is--very insulting to you and A.J., Sam doesn't really mean it as a personal insult. It's just part of the way he talks, like he might refer to someone as 'stupid' when they really aren't dumb. Expecting Sam to think before he speaks is like waiting for a dog to clean up after himself. It's not likely to happen anytime soon. In face, Guido accused Sam of abusing Italians and Sam just laughed it off and denied it."

"That's a bad habit that can get a fella into trouble," Joe replied. "Overall, I get the sense that Sam's nose isn't exactly clean, if you get my meaning."

"You're absolutely right, Joe," I affirmed. "I keep telling him that he'd better get himself straight."

"Exactly how did he get enough money to buy out the previous owner of the company?" Joe wanted to know.

I shook my head. "Oh, good grief, that's a story in itself. See, Sam had been employing three guys from one of the State schools for 'compromised' people. You know, they had mental disabilities that kept them from getting regular jobs. The State paid Sam to give them doable work and room and board and a small paycheck."

"And Sam started pocketing that money for himself and not paying them," Joe suggested.

"Spot on," I agreed. "Worse yet, you guys gave him some money for the business, right? Well, during that time, I was going through paperwork one day, and I discovered that Sam was keeping two sets of books. The bastard was skimming off the top. I told him he couldn't get away with that and to stop it immediately."

"Why, that double-crossing son of a bitch!" Joe exploded.

I lifted my hand. "It's not happening anymore, Joe. I told him he would be dead in a short time if he kept it up, and I guess he believed me, because he stopped doing it. And I've been keeping an eye on everything--the cash flow, invoices, bank accounts, the whole ball of wax. He's managed to put all the skimmed money back where it belongs. You needn't worry; it's all open and aboveboard now. But--" I grimaced.

"But what?" Joe looked at me.

"Oh, that whole company is so fucked up, pardon the pun. Sam is screwing his secretary, whose husband works close by at the apple processing plant. And Stefano, who handles a lot of the business and is kind of a right-hand man to Sam--well, he's screwing one of the women who work on the line right there at our food-processing plant. Between the two of them, I'm surprised anything related to business ever gets done."

"Are there any new business prospects in the offing?" Joe inquired.

"Well, Stefano and I went to a meeting recently with some Canadian guys who were looking for pre-made salads, potatoes, and other perishables that could be kept stable during shipping long enough to get to their wholesaler."

"What happened?"

"We just couldn't meet their terms," I explained. "I guess they went back to Canada and figured out how to do it all on their own up there."

"Too bad; it sounds like it could have been good for business." Joe sympathized. "Well, all I can say is, you'd better do what you can to convince Sam Fields that calling people *'Guinea Wop'* is very offensive and he might not be so lucky next time."

"You got that right, I agree completely," I told Joe, while privately vowing to come down on Sam as hard and convincingly as I could on the issue.

Later that day, I stopped by Joe's office and told him I'd be making a collection that evening. Joe said, "Well, like before, Stan will give you whatever you need. And if you need cash for anything, just speak up; whoever's around will give it to you."

My collection that night was another success. The bull work was accomplished without resorting to actual violence and the bill was paid in full and then some. I brought the extra cash to Stan, just as before, and again, he told me to keep it.

The next day, when I saw Joe, he handed me an envelope. "You're doing really good work, Chris. Take this."

He didn't have to tell me twice; I slid the envelope into my pocket. Then Joe and I left to go on some errands. When I finally got to peek into the envelope, there were five one-hundred dollar bills in it.

Clearly, I was being rewarded for having helped to prevent a major incident from happening. I knew that if A.J. had actually shot Sam, it would have (pardon the pun) triggered a huge scandal and put the Mob out front in the local news. So, I felt really good about my accomplishment, and, as usual, the extra money didn't hurt a bit. My young daughter had been talking every day about wanting a pony, and now I could probably make that happen.

CHAPTER FIFTEEN

While I helped Joe's little group avert a disaster, the shootings that had previously taken place, including those of *Samuel J. Russotti, Norman Huck, Enrico Visconte*—and later, Billy Lupo—had put Frank Valenti in the hot seat. So, he made some moves to distract the attention being received from law enforcement by orchestrating a series of bombings on public buildings in Rochester. These are now recognized as a master plan dubbed "The Columbus Day Bombings."

In 1970, Frank Valenti met with Buffalo Family Boss Stephano Maggadino, and told him that the Rochester Family's allegiance was switching to the Pittsburgh Family. Maggadino was helpless to do anything to stop Valenti, because his own health was failing and he was struggling with dissention in his own Family. Rochester would operate from then on as an independent Family, with Maggadino continuing to collect 15% of the gambling revenue.

The problems generated by the increased underworld activity in Rochester didn't escape the attention of law enforcement and the media there. Valenti struck back when the local publicity became too much to bear. Gang member *Eugene DeFrancesco* assembled several bombs. These explosives were created for two reasons: one was to intimidate some of Valenti's enemies, and the second reason, even more important, was to distract law enforcement officials from his unlawful operations.

Two black churches, the Federal Building, the County Office Building, and a union official's home were hit in the first round. A couple of weeks after that, two synagogues were it, followed days later by another synagogue. Then, a few weeks later, the home of a Monroe County Court judge was the target. The timing was perfect; the bombs were detonated in the early morning hours of October 12, 1970, hence their being dubbed the "Columbus Day Bombings."

This distraction proved very useful to Frank Valenti. The heat was off the Mob, at least temporarily and there was time to strategize further. Pleased with these results, Frank arranged for more such distractions, and six more explosions were set off between October 27 and December 14. The targets for those bombings were three synagogues, a Black Islamic mosque, a Black Baptist church, and also the home of a county court judge. The nature of Valenti's targets were surely the work of radical groups, Vietnam War protestors, and other discontent militants--or so it was believed. Thus the attention of the law enforcement brigade slid away from the mob and focused primarily on the bombings rather than the ever-increasing elements of organized crime in the city.

Looking back at some of this violence and upheaval in Rochester, I'm amazed how Joe and Stan virtually shielded me from most of it. While I began to have my suspicions about the people actually behind those bombings, I didn't hear anything definitive from anyone within our group. (I was out of the Mob before June 1975, when a federal investigation finally revealed the truth behind the bombings.) And my own personal convictions about being better off not knowing much definitely saved my sorry little ass on many occasions. I kick myself almost every day for having been part of such a bloodthirsty, heartless bunch, but hindsight's always 20-20 and I sure didn't have it then.
# # #

Another successful collection I recall involved a bowling alley, of all things. The establishment would not pay its bill to the produce company I worked for. I went there to collect the payment two or three times, and Angelo, the owner/manager would go hide when he saw me coming.

So, I went to Stan and told him about it, and he said to take a car and however many men I needed. I told him I would go late at night with two guys to back me up, and he barked, "Go for it!"

When we arrived there, Angelo saw me walking over towards his office and he tried to run out the back door. He didn't get very far because my men were there. They had a very intimidating presence. Then Angelo started blurting out that he could send a check "next week."

"Nope, that won't work. I want cash--now!"

I let him see the .45 tucked in my waistband, but I didn't pull it out. Evidently just the sight of it made him fear that we were going to hurt him physically, and I assured him we would if he didn't pay up right now. I pointed to that .45 and insisted he give us the money owed to my company right then. I also told him, "You're going to pay extra for my helpers and for my having to come over in person so late at night to collect what should already have been paid. This evening time is supposed to be mine to spend with my family, not for chasing bad debts."

As he counted out the cash, I informed him that our business with him would be on a cash basis all the time from now on--no more charging or credit. "And, don't try switching to another supplier, or you'll wind up dead."

I put my hand on the .45 to make sure he got the point.

Angelo spluttered and stammered, "Oh, no, no, of course not. Thank you." He sighed and wiped off the sweat now pouring down his face. In a few minutes, he had pulled together the necessary cash and we were done. I gestured to my henchmen, and they walked over to me, scowled very pointedly at Angelo, and then we all went out the front door. I heard the lock click into place behind us.

As usual, I reported my success to Stan the next morning, and, as usual, he told me to keep the extra cash. Woo-hoo!

Then there was an incident with a customer of my employing produce company, named Darrell. He owned a restaurant in a great location and had a thriving business. We delivered produce and other items the company carried to his establishment every Monday, Wednesday, and Friday. His account was on a charge basis, to be paid in full each month. Suddenly, his account was in arrears and he didn't want to pay it. I tried stopping in during the busy lunch hour and he'd make excuse that his checkbook was at home.

"Gosh, I'm sorry, Chris," he told me. "I'll try to remember to put a check in the mail just as soon as I get home."

I returned to my car but didn't drive away; a few minutes later, I saw him leave the restaurant and I followed him home. When he arrived there, I pulled in the driveway right behind him. Darrell was angry and started spouting off at me, but I let him see my ever-present .45. I told him that I wanted all of the money he owed plus interest.

"You'll be wise to pay me right now," I emphasized. "And from now on, you're going on a cash basis with our company. If you know what's good for you, you'll get that money now and keep things straight with us."

Darrell decided that compliance might save his sorry ass, so he paid every cent of what was owed--or, rather, what I demanded.

Shortly after that incident, I found out that Darrell was running for some public office in his district. So, Joe, Stan, and I showed up at his restaurant for lunch. That evidently had the desired effect, which was to scare the hell out of Darrell. He was very surprised to see me in easy, close company with such powerful men. His chances of being elected would be zero if it was rumored that he had ties to the Rochester Mob. He fell into line very quickly and there was no further trouble with him.

"Ya did a really good job with him, Chris. You're a natural at collections, never seen anything like it!" Stan praised me.

"Absolutely, great job." Joe agreed.

# # #

I don't think I've mentioned my old friend, Hank, much up to now. Hank and I had known each other since way back in our high school days. The two of us had been through thick and thin, and our families used to get together for kids' playtime, picnics, and other activities.

Hank's one of those guys whose critical thinking skills are pretty minimal, although at one time he was an ambulance driver and EMT, and delivered his share of babies while enroute to a hospital. He even knew Frank Valenti; they sometimes hung out in the same bar and Hank referred to him by the "Uncle Frank" moniker. Sure, Hank was able to think out some things. But he also liked playing the role too much and throwing his weight around, and he didn't handle power very well. He's the type who'd shoot first and ask questions later.

Me, I'm more analytical and am constantly looking ahead, evaluating exit strategies, etc. I will admit that Hank and I had done a bit of intimidating and made a couple of independent bill collections of our own in the past, always with me taking the lead and him playing second fiddle. But it was way too risky to let him be in charge.

Now, as I began to gain a bit of personal power and money with the boys, Hank begged me nonstop to include him on some of the bigger collections. He just about went nuts when I hinted at the extra money I was making. But, I knew I couldn't let him in on anything very major. For one thing, he would never pass muster with the Mob, and for another, he had no leadership skills. And, he loved to brag and play the big-shot role. He'd have shot someone just for the hell of it and then yapped about it to anyone who'd listen. And, the boys would have crucified him without a second thought the first time he screwed up.

"Sorry," I told Hank, "I just can't do it. This is big-time shit and there's no room for a mistake or a hot head. I'm already at risk every day and the stress is killing me. I can't take on the responsibility for you, too. Sorry, buddy."

Hank was disappointed, but accepted my decision. He still hung on to every word when I dared to share a bit of the actions and excitement I was experiencing. But I never told him enough details to endanger anyone or compromise Mob activities. So, he just had to be contented with hearing my edited stories. Some time later, after I had left the Mob, we would carry out some collections together, but that was in the future.

Before that happened, I would learn that Hank had been boffing Norma when I wasn't around, but it took a while for that information to trickle down to me, the dumb, naïve trusting jerk that I was!

Meanwhile, the fun with the boys never stopped. It's a wonder I could keep up with my produce company job and still find time to work with Joe and Stan. Somehow, though, I managed.

One of my produce customers was a popular restaurant located on Route 104 near Webster. It was quite large and operated by a father and son team. The son had a speech impediment but was a good kid; he was somewhere around his early twenties. But the father, *Ciro*, got himself into trouble with his liquor suppliers. They put him on their black list, meaning that he had to pay cash for all of his liquor deliveries. That hurt him, big time, so he started switching suppliers and got into trouble with one of them, too. It happened that my "guys" happened to own it.

So, I went to the father/owner and told him I wanted extra money every week towards paying off that unpaid bill and that he was on a strictly-cash basis for all future deliveries from "us."

The following week I stopped by to get the money.

"Oh, I'll send them a check," he promised. When I spoke with the office a few days later, they told me that they had, indeed, received a check from him. The only trouble was, he'd made out the check to another company--a typical stalling tactic.

Well, he was messing with the wrong people. I returned to his establishment, bad check in hand.

"What's going on? I sent a check."

"Yeah, one we can't cash," I replied. Then I grabbed him by his shirt collar and told him he'd better keep his end of the bargain right now.

"If you don't, you and your son are both gonna get hurt," I got my face right next to his. "Is that what you want? Just keep fucking us over and you won't be around to tell about it!"

"Okay, okay, I'll work something out!"

Ciro doggedly scraped together the money to pay us a decent amount on his bill each month, until it was finally paid off. Not long after that, he went broke and left to go work as the cook in another restaurant. I saw him there, and he bragged, "You're the only ones who got any money from me. I kept a lot of cash back and stiffed those other guys. They'll never get another dime from me!" He laughed.

"You're damned lucky you don't still owe us anything," I replied. "Someone like you shouldn't be in business, you're too incompetent and greedy. What you're doing is very dangerous. Other people won't be as tolerant as my boys were."

That was a stupid comment, wasn't it? There was nobody greedier and less tolerant than the Mafia, but I played the role anyway ad consoled myself with the thought that I was being a good little soldier, just doing my job.
#

"Good morning, Chris," Joe greeted me one day. He and A.J. were in the office, going over some paperwork. Casually, Joe mentioned that he'd heard that so-and-so had been bumped off yesterday. He pointed out an article on the front page of the *Rochester Democrat and Chronicle* daily newspaper.

A.J. laughed. "Well, well," he commented. "So shit really happens."

"Amazing how that catches up to dirty rats," Joe actually smirked, while A.J. continually grinned.

I kept my cool and didn't let my inner reaction show. But my insides twisted into a knot. They'd just essentially told me that they'd rubbed out someone—an enemy—or knew who had, and thought it was funny. I kept my facial expression noncommittal and just mumbled, "Huh." I asked no questions and made no comments.

However, I momentarily reflected, in private how, over the past year, I'd noticed the outright disappearance of several individuals we'd formerly known or done business with there in town. One day the person would be around, and then he was gone, never to be seen again. I wanted to be sure I'd not be included in that lot, so I acted as though it was no big deal and showed no curiosity about it. But it scared me and kept me always on my guard and on my toes. These people were not to be messed with or jerked around, and no one knew that better than I did.

CHAPTER SIXTEEN

Summer had taken its time arriving in upstate New York, but it was finally my favorite time of year. My young kids were out of school and growing fast. I'd always tried to make time to do typical, summertime family stuff with them. Now, though, I was usually so busy with my produce sales job and duties with the Mob that I figured the only way I could keep up with everything was to never sleep. But then Joe and his "entourage" decided to throw a big family picnic. I'd have the weekend off, a very welcome prospect. The anticipated event gave my youngsters something to look forward to, and on the scheduled day, they weren't disappointed.

A huge city park on Lake Road near Pultneyville on the outskirts of Webster, NY was the site. It was in an expanse of land between Irondequoit Bay and Lake Ontario itself, but not directly situated on the water either way.

On a warm day in July, though, it was the perfect spot to be. Huge trees provided shady spots and large picnic tents made for comfortable relief from the direct hot sun. The park also sported a baseball diamond, Jungle Gym play area, a large cookout/picnic pavilion, restrooms, etc. Huge expanses of trimmed green grass invited children to run their legs off; mine certainly took advantage of it. In fact, the entire event was set up specifically for children and their families. Costumed clowns added to the gaiety; they blew up balloons, painted faces, and engaged the kids in various games and activities.

This event was fully catered by professionals, and no expense was spared. Huge grills were set up in the picnic pavilion to cook hot dogs, hamburgers, chicken, sausages, and whatever else a guest might want. Naturally, there were tables of side dishes and traditional picnic food—delicious salads, top-brand potato chips, etc., and a fancy dessert table captured the attention of everyone. A portable bar was set up to dispense beer, wine, and whiskey; Joe had to have his whiskey! Soft drinks and lemonade gurgled down the thirsty children's throats by the gallon. All in all, it was quite an extravaganza, and my children recalled it fondly for many years afterward.

Naturally, Joe never let down his guard. There were a half-dozen "toughs" at the main park entrance, to prevent any outsiders from coming in. Huge "Reserved" and "Private Party" signs were set at every entrance and exit point. Quite a few more street-attired toughs I knew wandered around discreetly keeping an eye on things. To ensure a quick getaway if such a thing were necessary, Joe's and A.J.'s cars, particularly, were backed in closely to the pavilion. Joe was always nervous about being so out in the open, and was very careful to leave himself a quick exit.

I should mention that Joe, A.J., Stan, and other key figures were very strict about their use of language when women and/or children were anywhere near. Even "hell" and "damn" were never used--not once--and the henchmen and other soldiers and associates followed that example. I respected their restraint and adhered to it myself, at least in public situations.

Joe and his wife and two young-adult children attended the picnic. So did A.J. and his wife; they had two small children. It always impressed me how A.J. and his truly beautiful lady made such a striking couple. Picture a handsome, 30'ish Al Pacino and the late Natalie Wood and you'd know what I mean—an attention-attracting pair. (Yes, I know that Ms. Wood was actually of Russian heritage, but anyone who'd seen her in the original "Westside Story" film would swear that she was Italian. A.J.'s wife had that kind of beauty.) As usual, both A.J. and his wife were both impeccably dressed; she had great taste but did not flaunt her body like someone else I knew.

Oh, who would that be? Norma and I and our kids joined in an exuberant soccer game there at the picnic. My once demure and fairly low-key wife had become quite the showoff of her shapely size 6 or 8 body. I can't remember exactly which it was, I just know it was worth a second or third look, if you know what I mean. With her pretty smile, brown hair and eyes, clad in her favorite tight white shorts and a light blouse, she already garnered attention. Then she shed the blouse "because it was too warm," making her perky cleavage evident in an abbreviated halter top.

Naturally, I was proud of having such an eye-catching wife, but then she came over to me and complained that our Market Mob cohort, Mustache, had hit on her. Granted, he'd been drinking, unlike me; Joe had specifically told me to stay straight "just in case." As she repeated his words, I bristled. I didn't like what Mustache had said to Norma, and was going to take it up with Joe the next chance I got.

Meanwhile, I woke up a little; my mind came on, sober and strong. I suddenly realized that Norma was being a little too free with flaunting her body out of the privacy of our own home. This was all the more true since I was pretty damned certain that she was screwing around on me, and had done so more than once. But that damned pedestal kept getting in my way and blocking my view of reality.

Even so, privately, I told her, "You're going to cause a problem some day, strutting your stuff like that. It's not really appropriate."

I guess I must have come off to her as confused, because while I was chiding her for her "over-exposure," I also was digging it as much as the next guy--and of course, she knew it, as she knew all my weaknesses. Talk about being pussy whipped; I was putty in her hands.

Wide-eyed, Norma smiled and then laughed. "What's the matter, don't you like it? After all, I'm doing it for you. I thought you liked having a sexy wife."

Of course I did, and told her so. And, I was too dumb and naïve then to realize that she really wasn't showing it off for my benefit. She still walked on water in my heart and mind's eye, but I was more and more aware that she was looking for attention from any man who'd look her way and like what he saw. But I just couldn't see the forest for the trees, I guess.

Worse yet, in the not-so-distant future, it would finally dawn on me that, after that picnic, Norma had been recruited by the Mob to perform in sex videos and engage in private sex parties that paid handsomely. At this particular event, other Mob guys besides Mustache who were at the picnic were also taking note of Norma's "charms" and filing their impressions away for future reference. This included the guys I worked for: Joe and A.J. Behind my back, they were profiting from my wife's willingness to fuck anything that walked. They were quietly "recruiting" her with me being none the wiser.

But, blissfully unaware of this undercurrent involving my wife, I tried to enjoy myself, and thought that the rest of the picnic went well. The kids were thrilled but exhausted and all fell asleep in the car on the way home that evening. But I didn't sleep all that well.

On the next day at the Market, I sat down with Joe and said, "I've got a bit of a problem. You may not have noticed, but at the picnic, Mustache was hitting on Norma. He made some pretty vulgar comments about her figure and how he'd like to 'do her,' and it really pissed me off. I just want you to know, because I'm going to talk to him."

It's weird; this story is supposed to be about my time with the Mob, and yet it all keeps coming back to sex, doesn't it? If I'd known then what I know now, I'd have saved my breath. And I wouldn't have been so damned dumb as to think my wife wasn't planning and carrying out her own private agenda. "To love and honor" was a wedding vow I'd made seriously and I'd never dreamed Norma would be the first one to break it. Or that I would eventually break it, too.

Meanwhile, Joe kept a straight, totally believable face and shook his head. "Not your job, I'll take care of it," he told me, and he sent someone out to track down Mustache who was working there in the Market. When Mustache walked into the office, Joe lit right into him. In fact, he put the business end of a .45 against his head.

"Chris tells me that you were hitting on his wife at the picnic."

"Aw, it was no big deal. I was drinking a bit, feeling good, and who doesn't appreciate a good-looking dame who's stacked like Norma?"

Joe clicked the hammer back on the .45. "You know the rules. We respect family and don't get insulting or vulgar with wives and kids. You're lucky not to be going out of here in a body bag today."

Mustache appeared to be appropriately frightened. "Yeah, okay, I got the message. Sorry, Chris, no hard feelings, okay? You're one lucky guy. I got your meaning, Joe, please put that thing down!"

Joe put away the handgun. "Okay," he said, "But this better not happen again. We don't like it and won't have it."

Mustache couldn't get out the door fast enough.

"Thanks, Joe. I was just going to tell him I didn't like it. But, boy, you sure got the message across a lot better. I appreciate that."

"Not a problem. Now, I need to get to a meeting over at Ben's, so let's grab the Lincoln and go."

Wow, I thought to myself; it's really nice to have friends in high places! Joe's threat to Mustache had scared me even though that gun wasn't pressed to *my* head. That looked pretty scary and seemed to be spontaneous. These guys are really supportive and great, I smiled to myself.

I thought that would be the end of a connection involving sex with Norma and the Mob. But, in the back of my mind, something wasn't quite right. I would later remember this encounter and then suddenly flash on another incident involving Mustache at that picnic event. However, since there was so much going on right then, my mind just filed it away someplace in its "deal-with-this-later" spot.

I also realized, in hindsight, that it was after the picnic when Norma began to subtly pull away from me, to become a bit distant and more independent. Now, was that normal? No. Where was *Star Trek's* Mr. Spock and his pet phrase, "That's not logical, Captain" pronouncement? It was very applicable, but I didn't see it--yet.

CHAPTER SEVENTEEN

I could barely deal with life at the present, and had I known what was coming along in the not-so-distant future, I'd have dug a big hole, jumped into it, and pulled the grass over my head.

Still, life went on. I scored a real victory business-wise when I set up a meeting for all of the produce company's vendors. We sat and discussed bad customers we all had. Some of them would change companies and then the new company would call the previous supplier and ask about the customer's record. If the customer had been a slow or no-payer, then the new supplier would inform them that they'd be on a cash-on-delivery basis. This policy often meant that the customer would then revert back to the original supplier, but they'd still have to pay off their existing bill or they'd get no supplies. This practice was basically against the law and eventually we had to stop giving companies each other's information.

But the vendors had other ways of getting new accounts, such as by cutting prices on the products, or by overlooking the fact that some customers took to keeping double sets of books so they could cheat on taxes. This was not a good idea for what was basically a small-potatoes enterprise. The Mob could push their luck and get away with this monkey business for quite a while, but the average guy didn't have a prayer. He'd be caught and then financial ruin quickly followed.

One of our most memorable shakedowns involved a dry cleaning store on Clinton Avenue. The owner was tired of paying protection money anymore. He told me that he needed every cent he had to help out his sick mother and father from the old country. My bosses said to get the money from him, no matter what it took.

"Gee, Joe," I hesitated. "Couldn't we cut the guy a little break? I mean, he's trying to help his folks."

"I'd like to Chris," Joe responded. "But it wouldn't look good to all of the other people we shake down, and the Teams would be upset, too." (Most of the Rochester *Mafia* guys were on either the A Team or the B Team. We were part of the B team.)

"Okay, Joe. I'll take care of it." What else could I say?

When I went back to the dry cleaners, I told Vinnie to stay outside and keep on the lookout for me. That sounded legit, since the cleaners was one of those businesses right on the border of Mob territories.

Inside the shop, I asked the owner, "How much do you pay us each month?" I never checked those envelopes; I just turned them over to Stan or Joe.

He said that he was currently forking over $200 a month.

"Bring me an envelope," I ordered him. He complied, and I took $200 from my own wallet and placed it in the envelope. "That's all I can do," I said. "But I can't keep you safe after this."

Gratitude shown in the tired man's eyes. "Thank you, thank you very much. This help me much," he told me. "No worry; I pay each month after today."

I went back outside and casually said to Vinnie, "No problem, I got the money," and waved the envelope.

"Well, that's impressive, Chris," Vinnie congratulated me. "And no bloodshed, either, I take it?"

"Not a drop. Nice guy, he means well."

I never got that $200 back, but I didn't care. The poor guy needed it more than I did. And, I never told Joe about it, either. He was pleased that the man had apparently paid me without a hassle and the matter was closed.

# # #

I'd been making more and bigger collections over the months, and one day, I told Joe and Stan that my company was having trouble with the food service buyer at a large, well-known healthcare product manufacturer in the city. I described how the company had a large cafeteria for its employees, and bought produce and other food products, including canned goods. The orders were usually quite substantial, but lately, they hadn't ordered as much from us as usual. And, they were increasingly slow to pay.

"Oh, yeah?" Stan scoffed. "I know that outfit and I heard they've been scamming people. What and how do you know about it?"

"Well, I took an order in last Friday—they buy canned goods as well as fresh produce from us--and as I came in the door, I actually saw a competitor making a delivery. He handed Jim, the buyer, some money in a way that wasn't open and aboveboard, if you get my meaning. And, boy, was Jim nervous when he saw me! He knew I'd seen what took place."

"Hmm. That sounds like he's playing both ends against the middle. We don't like that and it's not acceptable. Okay, Chris, let me chew on this for a while. You check back with me later this afternoon, about 4:00, and I'll fill you in on what we'll do." Stan waved his hand in dismissal and I left.

After meeting later with Stan as directed and developing a game plan, I went home and spent the weekend with my family. The minute I pulled into the driveway, I put my suspicions about Norma in the back of my mind and tried to get through the weekend.

As usual, Norma and I got in as much hot sex as we could fit into the time. She was still smiling down on me from that damned pedestal she occupied in my mind. I just turned to Silly Putty whenever I saw her face, and resisting her charms was an exercise in futility. As any married couple knows, sandwiching sex into the scene when young children are around is usually difficult. Sometimes we had to grab a piece of ass when the kids were all outside playing and there were about ten minutes to spare. We'd lock the bathroom door; I'd lift up her short skirt and my cock would be in her within a minute. Norma was always ready to fuck and my testosterone was running high so we'd both get off in an orgasmic high. There, I would think, she's still mine and she really does still love me. What a moron!

Over the weekend, when there was a quiet moment, I got my head together in earnest for the coming business fun, Mobster style. This was going to be such a power trip, I knew, and I could hardly wait. It would make my previous collections look like child's play.

On Monday, I walked into the buyer's office at the healthcare product company. When Jim saw me, he tried to act nonchalant. I cut right to the chase, but in a way that caught him off guard.

"Hi, Jim. Nice day, isn't it? Say, we're going to be carrying new products and have some great business deals going. Let me take you to lunch and I'll tell you all about them."

Jim looked at his watch and shrugged. "Well, it's close enough to noon, I guess. Sure."

We walked out to the dark blue Lincoln I'd left in the parking lot. As I pulled out into traffic, I said, "Jim, pull down that sun visor." I gestured to the visor just up above and in front of him.

He pulled it down and looked at the photograph clipped to it. The photo was of his three children. Jim stared at it and then over at me, his mouth hanging open.

"Yeah, those are your kids. We knew where they go to school, and where you live. We know they come home at 3:15 and that your wife is there to give them their milk and cookies. Your daughter has dance lessons every Tuesday at the Twirly Toes Studio and your son plays next door with the Johnson's kid."

The color was draining out of his face; I think he knew what was coming. But I spelled it out anyway, in no uncertain terms.

"See, Jim, we know that you're double-crossing us. I saw you take that kickback from our competitor last week. That's not okay. Now, you either play ball with us—and I'll tell you how in a minute—or you won't have a family to go home to. It's that simple.

"From now on," I told him, "your department will generate a produce order for a certain amount each week. Your secretary will telephone that order in to us every Tuesday, without fail and without any exceptions. You got that?"

Jim was visibly shaking. "I-I-think I—"

"What's that? You don't get the picture? Shall I describe it to you in detail, what will happen to your wife and kids? It won't be painless and it won't be quick."

"God, no, no, don't do anything to them! I'll make sure that order is phoned in every Tuesday, you can count on that. Only, please don't hurt my family!"

"Okay, Jim. I want to take you at your word, so it better be good." Then I looked at my watch. "Gee, where did the time go? I won't be able to take you to lunch after all. We'll just go back to your office. I know you have lots of work to do," I finished, looking him full in the face. "You have some phone calls to make and people to talk to," I suggested.

"Er, yes, yes, I do." Jim's hands were trembling.

"Now, don't forget the arrangements. The orders need to total at least 40 cases of canned goods a month, plus the fresh produce. And we'll be watching, so don't try anything funny, like complaining to someone about this. Remember, we know where you live," I reminded him.

"Absolutely!"

Jim stepped out of the Lincoln the minute we stopped in the parking lot. His shirt was soaked with sweat and his color was terrible. He'd gotten the message.

I reported back to Stan and Joe.

"Good job!" They both gave me a back pat and a handshake. "Just keep us posted if that guy forgets to keep his end of the bargain," Stan told me.

As I drove home that evening, I marveled at the ever-increasing personal power I was acquiring. But it was at a terrible cost. I'd always been a fairly nervous, anxious person, and now that every day brought some new adrenaline rush, it was taking a toll. I wasn't getting enough sleep, hardly any healthy relaxation, and my little family was starting to fall apart. More than once I'd recently caught my wife in yet another compromising situation that smacked of infidelity. But I still didn't want to think about it. I'd been so much in love with her and just the sight of her soft brown eyes, long brown hair, and knockout figure convinced me all over again that there was nobody else for me. I know--it sounds like a continuous loop tape, doesn't it? Dumbshit still doesn't get it, keeps ignoring everything out of blind love. That was me.

Unfortunately, our children were showing signs of inadequate supervision at home and were acting out at school. On several occasions, I'd had to hurriedly drive to the kids'grade and run interference with the teachers. I'd been buying our children all kinds of indulgences and material things, but that wasn't making up for my physical absence as their father on a daily basis. They were starting to be mouthy and were acquiring what's now called the "entitlement mentality" to boot.

So, the home scene was a far cry from the white-picket-fence bliss I'd once imagined it would be.

Oh, well, life still went on and I was due for a chance at straying, myself . . .

About a month before the big party, Joe said, "Hey, Chris, we're having dinner and playing cards tonight at the One-Eleven. It's a little party of sorts. I'll need you there with me until about midnight." Joe mentioned. "This is a kind of thank-you function for you and the other guys we know and work with. It's our way of letting them know we appreciate them."

"Sure thing," I replied.

This ought to be interesting, I thought. Knowing how Joe and the others threw money around like water, I envisioned lots of cash changing hands in a card game that involved the Mob. I loved to play poker but didn't dare if I was drinking--which was most of the time.

The One Eleven on East Avenue was an establishment that did double duty as a sometimes-open-to-the-public nightclub; other times, it was privately booked as a party house. This was one of the latter occasions.

Joe, A.J., Mustache, some other bodyguards, and I all arrived early and enjoyed a good dinner. It was a place where I could actually sit and enjoy my meal, since the place was closed to the public and there was less likelihood of an ambush or other trouble. I didn't have to keep one hand on my gun every minute.

Soon, other people arrived. There were quite a few notable Mobsters present that night, not the least of whom was "Sammy G," who I've mentioned before. He ran his own crew, always looking for recognition, and showed no fear of anything. Frankly speaking, Sammy did his best to imitate Stan Valenti, but fell short of the mark. He was fairly tall, with a strong build, and was always dressed to the nines in expensive clothing. I didn't speak to him unless he specifically addressed me.

Privately, I considered Sammy G to be just one more gangster wannabe. People who have to excessively flaunt and posture the way he did aren't really due the respect of the genuine thing. It was a case of "some cats got it and some cats ain't," as the saying goes. However, one thing I'd been quick to learn was that, since respect was always mandatory to show, I wasn't to approach *anyone* without receiving a word or nod of recognition. That would be disrespectful.

And, to Sammy, who was moving up the ranks during this period, I was just another Mob associate. There was that old distinction of how I couldn't receive "soldier" status because I wasn't of Italian descent. Because of that, he probably didn't especially respect or appreciate my existence, but at least he tolerated my presence.

Soon, I discovered that dinner, drinks, and gambling weren't the only perks being offered that evening. This was hinted at when our pre-dinner drinks were served by a bevy of lovely, youngish women wearing very abbreviated outfits. All of them had gorgeous curves and enticing smiles. They were open and friendly, and made sure their shapely assets were revealed as they leaned forward to put down drinks and then swiveled away again.

There was something for everyone's tastes—blondes, brunettes, and redheads. Even a couple of knock-out-pretty black women with equally stunning figures worked the room. That was rare; very few blacks make it into the Mob or their activities. But that wasn't to say that some of these men didn't like a bit of brown sugar now and then.

Although I wasn't technically "working," I didn't consume much alcohol; I mostly stuck to soft drinks. Even so, it was impossible not to be interested in those pretty girls, and I found myself idly thinking it would be fun if I could get into bed with one or two of them. Norma and I had been fighting again over sex and money—nothing new there. But, at that point, I was always looking out for Joe and stoically kept my mind on protecting him "just in case."

After dessert was served, staff began clearing the tables, removing all of the coverings and tableware and setting them up for card games. Basically, everyone was there except Stan Valenti, and we were waiting for him to arrive.

Suddenly, the door to the room opened and one of Stan's bodyguards stepped into the room and quickly looked around. He turned and nodded to someone behind him; then Stan stood in the doorway.

Just like a scene from a movie, everything in that room stopped as if on cue. Wine being poured stopped mid-stream, cigarettes held in fingers waited for a lighter flame, conversation ceased, and the room was dead silent.

This happened in the fraction of a second. I'd never seen anything like it. All eyes were on Stan. He looked around and lifted his hands, palms up, in a brief, "So what?" gesture. As his hands fell, movements and conversations resumed immediately and everyone visibly relaxed.

Still mesmerized by the sight of that powerful man, I watched Stan approach a table of important dignitaries. The mayor and police chief both greeted him and another man stood and reached over to shake Stan's hand. I'd not noticed him before, but before my story in this book ends, I'd see him again, rather close up and personal.

Ties had been worn for dinner, but most were yanked off when the tables were cleared. The atmosphere was relaxed and comfortable. I stood behind Joe at one of the gaming tables. The opening ante for playing poker was a minimum of $5,000. So, right from the start, for a four-handed game, $20,000 lay on that table. I'd never seen that kind of money all in one place, especially for a card game, in my life! Players changed from table to table. There were quite a few local big shots there, including the mayor. Stan did not play at our table but I could see him laughing and challenging his poker partners. As usual, I stood directly behind Joe's chair while he played cards.

Eventually, Joe stood up. "I'm taking a break. Chris, you go ahead and mingle and enjoy yourself. There are rooms available upstairs, so if you want to—" Joe angled his head towards a couple of the young ladies. I'd noticed several "couples" pairing up and heading towards the elevator, and I wondered if some hanky-panky was going on in the guest rooms. Well, now I had my answer.

Hmm, what to do, that was my question. As I refreshed my soft drink at the bar, one of the women approached me. She had pretty brown eyes and soft brown hair, not unlike my wife. I'd have pegged her to be fortyish, a few years older than myself, but in very good form and sporting a nice tan. The lime-green sequined outfit she wore displayed ample cleavage, and her dazzling long legs were encased in black fishnet stockings. I could smell her expensive perfume and my mind began to persuade my body to consider honoring its wishes. In a word, I was quickly getting turned on by the prospect of hitting the sack with her.

"You look bored and lonesome, Honey," she murmured. "My name's Cindy. Shall we go someplace more private and get better acquainted?"

Momentarily, I thought of Norma, but not for long. A few days earlier, I'd come home and found her (again!) in pretty compromising circumstances with a guy I vaguely knew from the neighborhood. Norma had been half-dressed and he was hurriedly tucking in his shirt. They'd both denied any wrongdoing and made some flimsy excuses, but I wasn't born yesterday. The smell of sex was in the room. While I'd outwardly accepted the incident and wanted to give Norma the benefit of the doubt, I subconsciously knew that things had gotten very bad at home. Everybody was enjoying life but me, and that reality was getting really, really old.

I turned to Cindy. "Sure, let's go." We walked over to the elevator and rode it up a couple of floors.

"Here we are. What did you say your name is?" Cindy asked as she unlocked a door and we went into one of the graciously-appointed guest rooms. It sported a big, lonely looking, king-sized bed that could do with some company.

I told her my name and sat down on the edge of that bed. She looked at me carefully, and asked, "What's the matter, Chris?"

She bent down and untied my shoelaces. I was staring at her firm, pretty breasts pushing up over the top of her low-cut outfit. They were just begging for a touch.

"Well, I've—I'm married," I mumbled, holding up my left hand so Cindy could see my wedding ring.

"That's not unusual, Chris. Most of the guys I spend time with are married. It just goes with the territory. Is this the first time you've, uh, cheated on your wife?"

She sat down beside me on the bed and opened a package of condoms.

"Yeah, it is." I hung my head. "I know that my wife has been cheating on me, though, but some of that's my fault. I haven't been home much lately and she's a highly-sexed woman and wants more than I've been giving her, if you know what I mean."

To get the focus off myself for a moment, I looked into her pretty eyes. "Why are you in this, um, business? You're such a lovely woman. And you don't have a husband at home, waiting for you?"

Cindy shook her head. "No, I've had a couple of disastrous relationships and, frankly, I'm tired of hassling with guys and struggling so hard to pay the bills. Living costs a lot of money. A girl can't make much on her own—at least, not safely—so that's why I work these gigs for the Mob. They pay really well, a reputable doctor checks us over regularly, and no one is allowed to rough us up. It's much safer than working the streets or trying to find our own clients."

As she finished speaking, Cindy leaned over and her lips found mine. The tingle of that contact was electrifying. Then she set the condoms aside and started unbuttoning my shirt.

"Chris, we don't have to use these. I have them for one-time questionable strangers but I take the pill so I can't get pregnant. You're different." Her fingers pulled down my zipper and I gasped as her hand stroked my swollen penis.

That lovely woman kissed me again with those sizzling lips, and soon I was breaking my marriage vow of fidelity, with great enthusiasm. She was so hot, and I lost myself in passion and pleasure.

Eventually, I looked at my watch. "I have to get back downstairs, Cindy. Not that I really want to . . . but if I want to keep my job, it's what I've gotta do."

"Sure, I understand. I wish you all the best, Chris. See you around sometime?"

"Who knows?" I replied.

In the future, I would see Cindy again at other gatherings, but never again in such close proximity. Damn!

CHAPTER EIGHTEEN

The day of the big "party" had finally arrived. I'd been with the Mob for over two years now, and had been given quite a bit of responsibility for organizing what would ultimately be a big entrapment event for many local officials.

It took over a month to tend to all of the planning and details. Joe called me into his office and explained the sequence of events and what I was assigned to do. First, he gave me a list of people to contact—videographers, catering managers, and miscellaneous service providers. Last but not least was the name of a "Madame," the manager of an escort firm in Pennsylvania. Most of the other arrangements could be made by telephone, but I was to make a personal visit to her office.

Joe had a list of the invitees for this bash, which would be held in a large banquet hall at the One Eleven, which offered hotel guest rooms on several floors above the restaurant facilities.

"There'll be 80-100 people invited," Joe told me. "We're going to have a nice presentation from a guest speaker about new enterprises and business opportunities here in Rochester. He'll be speaking during dinner. So, plan for that many people when you organize the catering part of it. If some don't show, it's no big deal, we'll just give away any leftover food to a charity."

He went on to explain that we'd be using the same firm that had catered the big summer picnic in Webster. "They're good and easy to work with," Joe smiled. "They know exactly what to do and how to put out a good meal. Tell them we want a choice of three meat entrees; this will be a formal, sit-down dinner with all of the trimmings. The bar stuff will be separate; I'll work that out with the One Eleven. They're part of our organization and will do as they're told."

Ah—so that was it! I'd wondered how it was that the One Eleven had been so cooperative and knowledgeable about working with the Mob. It hadn't been by accident, but rather by design. This made me have all the more respect for the Family; they really had their fingers in a lot of pies and were very powerful there in the city.

Speaking of the Family, they naturally had their own stable of women available for sexual fun at any time. They were on the local payroll. When I mentioned this to Joe and asked why we wouldn't use them for this function, he shook his head.

"No, Chris, we need some superb, non-local girls that the cops here don't know. We don't want any familiar faces at this function; it's all part of the plan. This isn't just some low-level porno party like you went to a while back. It's a whole different ball game. What's going to happen is that a bunch of very foolish, big-wig guys are going to make bad choices, all to our gain. And those pretty, out-of-town ladies will be the key to our success."

So, very early one morning (3:00 a.m.!), I drove from my home to the familiar garage on Main Street. One of the other chauffeur/gofer guys, Vince, met me there. I had a key to the garage but he didn't. Joe had told me to take one of the Lincolns, so we climbed into the car for the drive to Scranton, Pennsylvania.

Joe had already set up an appointment with the escort service "Madame" to expect our arrival that day. We eventually arrived at the office suite, part of a larger business center, and walked in. It was a very nice, tastefully decorated suite. After we identified ourselves to the receptionist, we met Sheila. She was an attractive, hard-boiled looking woman, probably in her early 50's.

"What can I do for you?" Sheila asked. "I understand from Joe that you need our services for a specific function."

I took the lead in the conversation. "Yes, we would like to book about 50 of your escorts for an overnight party. They will be expected to serve drinks, probably rotating in teams of five or six at a time. That way, the variety of available women will be more evident. You'll have one person in charge who'll coordinate everything, I've been told."

Sheila smiled. "Of course. Janet is well-qualified and knows exactly what to do. She'll work with you to make sure everything meets your needs."

"Good. Please make sure that all of the escorts dress in such a way as to show off what they have. There will be a couple of tables of guys whose attention particularly needs to be concentrated on the girls."

Here, I was referring to the mayor and the police chief, who were usually as thick as the thieves that they were. Rumor was it that the mayor especially liked a little brown sugar, so there would need to be at least a couple of women of color included in the group.

It felt weird to be saying such things and having this kind of important role in facilitating high-class prostitution.

"You make sure to point out those special tables to Janet and she'll see that those guys can't take their eyes off what they see," Sheila smiled. "Would you like to see some of our escorts now?"

Vince and I looked at each other, trying to suppress grins of delight. We both nodded.

"Follow me." Sheila walked over to a closed door within the suite, and we found ourselves in a large room occupied about 15 women. They ranged around the room, chatting and laughing. There were blondes, brunettes, redheads, an Asian lady, and two black women.

I glanced at Vince; his eyes were nearly popping out of his head. All of the women were very scantily dressed and their assets were something to write home about! They ranged in age, I'd say, from about 23 to their early 30's. In a cold-blooded way, it was like walking into a meat market—only difference was, they made my blood run hot instead of cold!

It was a case of ooh-la-la; I knew exactly which woman I'd like to get together with back in Rochester at the party, if that became possible. Naughty, naughty boy!   Vince would later murmur his own preferred lady of choice to me, and we both mentally filed away our impressions for future reference. Meanwhile, we smiled and nodded to the women and went back out into the main office.

"Will they be satisfactory? The others are of comparable assets and looks, too." Sheila asked me. "I assure you, they'll all be the cream of the crop."

"Absolutely! No problem," I grinned.

We finalized the arrangements. I gave Sheila a cash advance of $6,000.

"Send them up to Rochester the day before the event so they can make themselves comfortable and get rested up in advance. We'll have nice guest rooms reserved for them," I explained. "Then they can go back home the morning after the party."

Sheila nodded. "Don't worry about a thing. As I said, Janet will be running the crew. You just show her where things are and she'll take it from there."

We shook hands and that was that. Vince and I got back into the Lincoln and drove back to New York.

That evening when we returned, Vince and I parted company at the garage. I went to the office to see Joe, and told him that everything had been arranged. Then I went home; I was bushed. It had been a long day with a lot of driving.

I had told my boss at the produce company that I would be away that day, prospecting some promising new clients out of town. And, I'd given Norma the same story. The fact that I was leading a double life was coming to be so prevalent that it was almost second nature to me now to lie to her and our friends. I'm sure that if some of them had known what I was *really* doing for a living, they'd have withdrawn and kept away from us. But, since I never came home in my Mob clothes and always drove the produce company station wagon with the logo on the side when I was coming and going there, they just saw me as another hard-working salesman, trying to provide for his family.

It was 4 p.m. on the day of the party. The invited guests began to arrive at the venue in the St. Paul Hotel. I saw the local police chief, mayor, and several other prominent dignitaries. This was the cream of the crop when it came to Rochester bigwigs: judges, district attorneys, the police commissioner, local politicians, and other elected officials walking through the door.

Janet's stable of girls was prominently on scene. They greeted each man at their assigned table and gave him their full attention while taking his drink order. They were supposedly servers with the food catering company, but their specialty that evening was going to be "dessert."

From a discreet vantage point, I observed the action in the room. The girls were flirting and making much over the men, and I saw more than one official's hand surreptitiously stroking a curvaceous thigh or buttock. In fact, the mayor couldn't keep his hands off the lovely dark-skinned woman serving him drinks along with plenty of assets showing. Rather than protesting this intimacy, the woman just smiled encouragingly and murmured, "Later" in a sultry manner.

Several times I wished that it was me sitting at one of those tables. But, since I knew why the women were there and what would ultimately happen, I had to stick strictly to the business at hand.

Soon, waiters appeared to take dinner orders. They scurried off to the kitchen and promptly returned with the desired food. Grilled beef steak tips, herbed chicken, and chunks of succulent grilled fish were served and enjoyed by the guests. The salads and other side dishes were perfectly prepared and attractively served.

During dinner, the regional keynote guest speaker had garnered attention with his presentation on new business opportunities for Rochester. I noticed several guests nodding to each other in agreement and enthusiasm about some of the information presented.

When the dinner plates were removed, a light dessert was served. However, I don't think much of it was eaten, because by then, the business presentation was over and the girls were back in full force to put the real dessert into action. They brought fresh drinks to the tables and started really hustling.

The two tables I'd pointed out to Janet received some extra attention; she'd selected a half-dozen of her most enticing escorts to serve those guests. And, what they didn't wear really showed off their gorgeous bodies. The guests were extremely appreciative of the attention and focused squarely on those beautiful women. Out of the corner of my eye, I noticed that the men had made their choices on which ones interested them the most.

The bartenders had been instructed not to make the drinks as strong after dinner; they were watered down. This was done to prevent the drinkers from overindulging to the point where they couldn't perform sexually, but they didn't know it. As those men continued to drink and ogle the women, they started feeling loose, that much anyone could see. It had been prearranged that anyone expressing interest in pairing off with one of the women would be encouraged to take her up to a guest room for some private attention.

With my own eyes, I saw those men—the police chief, the mayor, and a couple of city councilmen—leave the tables and disappear towards the elevators or the broad, carpeted staircase. When they returned anywhere from 30-60 minutes later, they were looking very happy, shall we say? A few looked nervous and quickly collected their coats and left the building. Others swaggered back into the room, cocky (great pun, huh?) with conquest and erotic pleasure. They lingered for another drink or two and chatted with their colleagues who'd remained at the tables.

Close to fifty percent of the attendees had given in to temptation and indulged in the extracurricular activities upstairs, I estimated. That ought to be good for something, I concluded, and I winked like a conspirator when Joe and I passed each other in the main room.

By 9 p.m., they'd all cleared out. I complimented the catering staff, tipped them, and privately paid Janet the rest of the fees owed for the escorts. Then I checked in with Joe, who appeared almost giddy and unable to stop smiling.

"We've got 'em in our pockets, now, Chris!" he gloated. "Good job, buddy. Go home now and get some rest. I'll see you in a day or so." He was obviously more than pleased.

I went home tired but happy that everything had gone so well. Everyone had done their jobs well, the food and drinks were perfect, and all the attendees appeared to have enjoyed themselves (some more than others, obviously). Knowing Joe, there'd be a big cash thank-you for me in a few days. Horny as hell from watching all of those sexy women strut their stuff, as soon as I walked in the door at home, I grabbed a stiff drink and then used something that was even stiffer for some fun with my wife.

When I next saw Joe, he had set up a video monitor in his office. "Take a look at this, Chris." He pushed in a videotape cassette and a moment later I was watching the action in some of the hotel rooms from the big party. Everything had been captured by hidden cameras in the rooms that meant those local officials and dignitaries were compromised by their balls, literally. Some of them were on top of the girls, fucking their brains out. Others had the woman sitting astride them, and several had their dicks being tongued and sucked. The mayor and police chief were both on there, in nice, clear images, going at it with the women like there was no tomorrow. It appeared that they both liked more than a little bit of brown sugar for dessert.

"See, Chris," Joe explained, his eyes dancing, "this is how we get law enforcement and other party poopers to look the other way and also to let us do what we need to do. They try to give us a hard time now, all we have to do is remind them that we have them being very, very naughty right on camera. Would they want the public to see them this way, to know that their elected officials are screwing whores instead of their wives? It's called 'moral turpitude,' among other things, and isn't something approved of by voters, to say nothing of wives and families. Suckers!"

"Wow!" was about all I could manage. I left the office with an extra $700 cash in my pocket that day, the expected "good-job-thank-you" and then some. Sweet!

Once again, the shrewd cunning and power of the Family came through, loud and clear. The old phrase, "Do you know who you're messing with?" applied in spades here. I couldn't get over how those stupid, elected officials would allow themselves to be so vulnerable as to engage in such scandalous behavior! It apparently never penetrated their thick brains that if something seemed too good to be true, it probably was. Boy, how they'd paid for their fucking with those broads. Now they were seriously compromised; their public credibility would be dashed to the rocks if these tapes were ever released for public consumption. Even just a hint of such scandal would, I knew, be enough to generate doubt and if the news reporters got wind of it, watch out! The shit would hit the buckwheat and it wouldn't be pretty.

As things turned out, it wasn't too long before the police chief and the mayor *were* both indicted on corruption and other charges. They gave up an awful lot, I concluded, just for pussy. Men never seem to learn; it pulls down both the best and the worst of them.

This was a truth I had learned before I turned 20—that sex and money are two extremely addictive aspects of life that can easily take control of a man, especially, and lead him to ruin. So can too much alcohol, which was causing problems in my personal life and decision-making process and it wasn't doing my health any good, either.

CHAPTER NINETEEN

"Sit down, Chris," Joe directed me. "I want to discuss an upcoming event that you'll need to attend, this time as a guest."

"Okay," I replied as I sat down across the desk from Joe. Probably another situation where he actually needed my protection as a bodyguard, I thought. Was I ever in for a surprise!

"As you know, we've put a lot of pretty important people in some rather compromised situations," Joe explained. "And, sometimes it's also in our best interests to provide certain 'rewards,' shall we say, to individuals who've helped *us* out of tight places."

Joe had my undivided attention and my antennae were up as high as they'd go. This sounded big.

"There's going to be a little party over at a pretty posh private residence owned by one of these special individuals. Now, he and his wife like their entertainment 'up close and personal,' you might say. The lady of the house is getting bored and her husband is only too happy to give her what she wants. The catch is, she needs a little extra something to ring her chimes." Joe's eyebrows waggled up and down and I caught his drift.

"O-kay," I responded slowly. "What does she need?"

"Well, she really likes sex, but she has to watch her husband socking it to another woman first. And that's where you come in."

I sat there silent, not sure what to say next. Was I going to be put out to stud, like a prize horse? Or was the husband such a stud he could do two women?

"I know you've said that your wife's quite a firecracker in that department and you're welcome to bring her along if she'd be up for it. *You'll* have to be there, one way or the other. If your wife doesn't want to participate, then you bring some other woman. And, whoever you bring needs to understand that she may be required to fuck the host."

It took me a moment to process this. I was required--not asked--to attend and probably participate in some kind of an orgy and they obviously preferred that I bring my wife. Ye gods! This was above and beyond anything I'd been doing for the Mob up to now. I needed more information and wanted to stall for time.

"So," I asked slowly, "would Norma and I be the only guests?"

"No, there'll be several other couples at the party, too. We just have no idea who the host will select as their partners, but it could be you and your wife so she'll need to go along with whatever he wants--if she decides to attend."

Joe sat back and waited.

I decided to play dumb. "And what about me? Am I just to be there for protection or what? You said 'partners.'" Smiling was difficult, but I tried to put on a brave face.

"No," Joe replied, looking me straight in the eye. "Actually, if the host selects your wife as his partner, then you'll be his wife's partner. Either way, whether it's some other woman you bring, or your wife, you could be required to perform--with the host's wife. Not coming to the party simply isn't optional for *you*."

For a moment, I was speechless. Also completely floored, flummoxed, shocked, sickened, and a few hundred other descriptors appropriate to the situation--there just wasn't one word that summarized it all. That's when I discovered how difficult it can be to think and respond clearly when your brain is on overdrive while your heart and soul are sinking like a torpedoed submarine.

"You okay, Chris?" Joe was leaning forward, looking me over carefully.

Finally I found my voice. "Yeah, yeah, I've just never done sex with an audience before. Guess there's a first time for everything," I finished, trying to smile and appear compliant, like a good little soldier.

"Good."

Joe sat back in his chair again. "That party is scheduled for two weeks from this coming Friday night. A limo will pick you up at a designated spot at 7 p.m. and take you home again later. Tell your wife--or lady friend--to go over to Victoria's Secret and pick out the sexiest underwear they have. Here's some extra cash."

Joe laid several hundred-dollar bills on the desk.

I picked up the money. "Anything else I should know?"

"Nope," he said. "That about covers everything. There'll be snacks and cocktails served, but don't drink too much in case you need to perform later."

I nodded. "Got it."

As I left Joe, my heart was very heavy; I knew that nothing would be the same after this upcoming "party." How could it be if both my wife and I had to have sex with other people while we were being watched? But I still had a family to support and didn't want my children to be made miserable by a weakness on my part. What Joe was asking was unthinkable and yet it was real. While Joe seemed to like and trust me, I knew he could be ruthless when it came to carrying out the Mob's business. I saw no choice but to go through with it and comply with his orders. Maybe, I thought, looking for a bright spot, we wouldn't be picked by the hosts. I had to keep that hope in mind.

That night, I went home and sat Norma down to explain the situation.

"You don't have to go to this party; I *can* take someone else. But if you do agree to it, you'll have to go along with whatever they want or we'll both be dead."

Norma wore a skeptical expression.

I looked her straight in the eye. "This isn't a joke," I emphasized, using a sterner tone than usual. "These guys don't accept refusals, so you couldn't suddenly change your mind at the last minute. And, if you do decide you'll go with me, you're supposed to go to Victoria's Secret and buy whatever you think is the sexiest stuff they have."

I put the money Joe had given me on the table. "They're even picking up the cost, so it's no out-of-pocket expense for us," I finished.

While Norma sat there thinking about everything I'd said, the dots were finally connecting in my overly-taxed brain. Well, duh! Joe and the party hosts had *already* pre-selected us! Otherwise, why shell out for expensive underwear for just one of the female guests? So the Mob was going to hire my wife as their whore for some bigwig to whom they owed a favor. And we couldn't get out of it, even if we wanted to.

Even so, I still secretly felt a bit duplicitous. I'd not mentioned the fact that I'd be required to "service" the host's wife if we were chosen to provide the "entertainment." And, it was obvious we'd already been preselected; this whole thing was carved in stone as far as Joe and the guys were concerned. But, I'd keep that information to myself, at least for the time being, especially since it obviously wasn't going to be a case of "if."

Unlike me, Norma had to have already known all of this, but she kept it to herself. She loved having her body seen by others and would just love an excuse to flaunt it in outrageously sexy underwear. That would be enough for her. Who cared who was fucking whom? That pissed me off all the more--she just couldn't wait to get with the guy. I assumed he'd be a stranger to her, which made the situation all the more repulsive to me. But, I had no choice but to play this game. Backing out would guarantee the end of my life, and for some reason I still valued the option to live. So, I would go along with the plan.

"Well," Norma finally spoke. "This is something you absolutely have to do--there's no choice, is that right?"

I answered her with an emphatic nod.

"And you have to bring along a woman; if not me, then someone else?"

"Yes." I looked her directly at her and played it straight, just as if I really thought she might decline to participate. "And I'll understand if you don't want to go. But I'm required to bring a woman, so I'll have to look up one of the broads I know who's connected with the guys and have her go with me."

"No way!" Norma raised her voice. "You're not going there with some other woman and play around with her."

"That's funny." I laughed. "If you go, you might be chosen to be the host's partner and have sex with *him*. And I'll probably have to watch. Why's it okay for you to do that but not for me to bring someone else?"

Somewhat testily, Norma snapped, "Because for me it would be something I couldn't say No to, right?"

Again, I nodded. "Yes. And I can't say "No" either way, so I don't have any privilege or choice. Look, Norma, the main issue here is that changing your mind at the last minute isn't optional. Once you're there, you *must* go along with whatever they want."

Always the gentleman, I played it through to the end, even though I didn't have to. I told her, "One thing you won't have to worry about is anything overly kinky or the least bit physically painful. Joe's got a high standard for not harming women and that includes during sex. He wouldn't allow anyone to slap you around or do something that would hurt."

Norma shrugged. "Okay. I guess there's no reason to not go." She picked up the money. "I'll go shopping in the next day or so, and make a note on the calendar about getting a babysitter for that night."

Was that a little satisfied smirk I saw on her face as she left the room? Talk about playing it straight; she was a master at the game.

As I walked away from the table, a sadness came over me. I was truly heartsick; I knew Norma had been cheating on me for a long, long time. And now, she was ready and willing to go fuck a complete stranger (or so I thought) with my full knowledge--and right in front of my face. The same might be required of me, but it wasn't my choice to go to this party.

Our marriage was collapsing and out of control. I was kind of surprised that we'd been able to discuss this newest twist in our lives without getting into the usual shouting match. That spoke volumes. She just couldn't get her panties off fast enough--no matter who the man was. So, when this upcoming caper was over, things were going to have to change--drastically.

I tried not to dwell on all of the aspects of upcoming life changes that party implied, but it was always in the back of my mind for the next two weeks.

##

Joe and I were having lunch at Ben's Cafe Society. This was a favored place for the guys in Rochester. A.J. soon walked in to join us, and so did Rene Piccarreto. I glanced around and saw Thomas Didio with a couple of other Mob guys. A moment later, the restaurant host led several patrons to a nearby table. Something familiar caught my eye--the long gorgeous legs of a pretty woman. When my eyes traversed up to her face, I almost fell over. It was Cindy, the lovely "professional lady" with whom I'd had an encounter after the card party back some time ago! She was laughing and talking with her male companion. Maybe he was a customer, maybe not.

I had a momentary pang of desire for her, because she'd sure shown me a good time that night we were together. And, I thought she was basically a very nice woman, not a hard-boiled bitch of a whore. But I took my eyes off her and turned my mind to focus on the situation at hand.

"Whatsa matter, Chris? You look like you just saw a ghost or something," A.J. chortled.

"Uh, no, I just remembered that I didn't mail something today. Damned bills never stop coming." I lied. "It bugs me when I forget important things like that."

"Aw, don't worry. Can't your wife take care of domestic shit like that?" A.J. put a forkful of lasagna into his mouth.

"Yeah, I'll call her and tell her to take it to the post office." I drank my iced tea and the conversation moved to something else.

My wife, he'd said. That cheating, lying bitch in whom I'd placed all of my dreams and hopes for happiness, the mother of my three children. And I was going to have to watch her have sex with another man in just a few more days.

I wanted to stop the world and get off. It seemed as though I just couldn't get away from sex for more than about five minutes. I felt like it was following me around or something, just waiting for me to give in to my carnal desires. It was true, though, that I was actually dreading that "command performance" party that was happening soon.

It wasn't my choice. Having sex with Cindy had been, and seeing her again was an unwanted reminder that my marriage was in failure, big-time, and that failure all fomented and churned around the subject and issue of sex. Damn that woman back home who'd introduced me to the pleasures of the flesh at such a young age, I thought. Sex been my downfall ever since. Were things going to stay that way forever?

CHAPTER TWENTY

It was the night that would end all peace for me. As Norma and I slid onto the seats of the limo, I realized that we wouldn't be able to see where we were going. The windows were all dark-tinted glass and the screen separating the front seat from the back obscured the view, especially since we'd been directed to occupy the seat facing the back. I tried to count the turns and get a general idea of the direction in which we traveled, but couldn't discern much.

But when we pulled into the massive garage at our destination, I could tell by the air and smell that we were somewhere very near Lake Ontario. Since I heard water lapping against the shore, it had to be some mansion right on the lake. I figured it might have been near the Crescent Beach area; even after all these years, that's what I believe. Plenty of well-heeled people lived there and many others patronized the well-known Crescent Beach Hotel.

We weren't allowed to linger in the heated garage, but were hustled through a door into the house. Once inside, I blinked rapidly to adjust my eyes. The main living room was very spacious and yet comfortable. While the decor wasn't opulent or ostentatious, the furnishings were obviously expensive and tasteful. Whoever owned the place had money, that much I could see. Interestingly, there was an absence of framed family photographs and other personal items that one would expect to see in such a home.

Uniformed serving people quietly took our coats. Norma was wearing an expensive but simple black silk sheath dress I'd bought her on an out-of-town trip. I wore a standard business suit and tie.

We were greeted by several other couples, and soon a waiter-type guy took our drink orders and directed us to a buffet table laden with what could best be descried as expensive heavy hors d'oeuvres. I spotted huge shrimp, smoked sausages, and other delicious-looking food. But my throat felt stuck shut; no way could I have swallowed a morsel. And, in keeping with Joe's advice, I stuck to a soft drink with plenty of ice that I could nurse for quite a while. Norma was never much of a drinker so she just sipped on a bourbon and cola.

Despite my nearly three years of being with the Rochester Mob, I didn't recognize any of the guests. Suddenly, we were being greeted by a new couple who turned out to be the host and hostess. They smiled and shook our hands, exchanging the usual pleasantries and welcoming us to their home. I looked the man full in the face and damned near dropped my pants. It was the guy I'd seen Stan Valenti talking to in that hotel ballroom back several chapters ago, the one sitting with the mayor and police chief during the frame-the-bigwigs party.

At the time I'd figured he was somebody important, like a judge or commissioner. The impression was still there. He was a good-looking Italian man in his early 50's or so, I figured. His name was *Piero*; he said to call him Perry.

His wife, Lucy--short for *Lucia*--was probably in her mid-40's and still had a *very* nice figure which was shown off by her expensively-tailored cocktail dress. She clasped my hand warmly and looked me full in the face, then her smile grew and her eyes sparkled like the diamond necklace she wore.

Uh-oh, I thought to myself. I'm being sized up as a potential sex partner. What if I don't make the grade?

I put my worries to one side as Norma and I were pulled into the gathering of other guests and we stood around making small talk. Gradually, some of the other guests began to melt away and I suddenly realized that Norma and I were the only ones left. Our host and hostess came up to us then, and invited us to "go see the rest of the house."

Norma and I followed them upstairs, admiring several sculptures set into alcoves along the hallway that had several closed doors. I actually wished I could just stay there in the hall, but there was no escape now.

"Norma, let me show you in here. Lucia, why don't you take Chris into the other room?"

Perry opened one of the doors, leading Norma into the room and closing the door behind them.

"Let me show you this room, Chris," Lucy directed as she opened another door.

We were in a large, tastefully furnished bedroom with a king-sized bed. Oddly, it was placed fairly close to a mirror-covered wall. Oh boy, I thought to myself. She wants to watch while we do it. But then how was she going to watch Perry when he boffed Norma?

That question was answered a moment later when Lucy shut off the light to the room we were in and touched a switch near the mirror. Suddenly, I realized that the mirror was actually a one-way window into the other room, which was fully lighted. Lucy touched another button and suddenly we could both see and hear Norma and Perry; they were in the next room. Their King-sized bed was fairly close to our shared wall, which obviously was mirrored like ours. Somewhere microphones were hidden in there. I noticed a couple of smaller mirrors were hung on the opposite wall of that room.

My misgivings must have been pretty obvious, because Lucy laughed and said, "Don't worry, Chris; we can see and hear them, but they can't see or hear us. Here, sit down and be comfortable."

In the other bedroom, we heard Perry say, "Here, why don't we sit down and get comfortable, Norma?"

He led her over to a red, velvet-covered loveseat and she sat, while he walked over to a table and poured himself a drink.

"What can I bring you?" Perry asked. Norma replied, "Nothing thanks," and smiled at him as he walked back over to the love seat.

Perry sat down beside Norma and put his arm around her in a familiar and affectionate fashion, and took a sip of his drink. He kissed her warmly, smiled at her, and then, without any hesitation, his other arm moved up and his hand clasped one of her breasts. He fingered and stroked it and then did the same to the other breast.

Norma responded to Perry as though they were familiar lovers, making sounds of enjoyment. Her hands caressed the back of his neck while they kissed. He, too, was caressing her; the kissing continued and it was passionate.

I couldn't believe how immediately Norma had started making out with Perry; it was as though they'd been together many times before. Then I realized that, without doubt, they were *not* strangers to each other. They behaved as familiar lovers do when they make love; this wasn't a random sexual encounter of two people. It was an anticipated, intimate sharing between a couple who knew and welcomed each others' touch.

In our room, I heard Lucy's quick intake of breath as the scene on the other side of the glass continued to heat up. Then she turned into a lusty cheerleading maniac.

"Come on, Perry," she exclaimed. "Go after those tits of hers--make 'em hard! I want to see them puckered and hard. Pinch them, Perry, pinch and suck them until she's all hot for your cock!"

Lucy and I were sitting a few feet apart on the bed. As she avidly watched Perry eventually strip off Norma's black dress, revealing the fancy underwear purchased at Victoria's Secret, Lucy became more excited. By the time he'd pulled off Norma's bra and panties, which were just scraps of lace, Perry had also removed his own clothing.

To my surprise, Perry then stood up and took Norma's fancy underwear over to the oak bureau, folded each piece carefully, and left them there. Most men don't do that and I thought it was quirky. Then he returned to the bed.

By now, Perry had a large, prominent erection, the sight of which galvanized Lucy into further action--with me.

"Come over here, Chris, come on over and play with my tits," she commanded.

As I complied, her fingers were expertly unbuttoning my shirt. I did as I was told, fingering her breasts and playing with them as she instructed me. But I was sick with heartache and revulsion. It was obviously not Norma's first time with Perry, I could see that and couldn't get the thought out of my mind. That made it difficult for me to show enthusiasm with Lucy, but I pretended to be as excited as she was.

As for Perry, he didn't seem to be in any hurry with Norma. Evidently, he knew exactly what Lucy wanted to see and how long it took her to become fully aroused--quite a while! I'd estimate he played around with Norma for a good thirty minutes, being egged on by Lucy, although he couldn't actually hear her. The whole event was evidently scripted in advance by the two of them.

Perry and Norma eventually moved into performing oral sex on each other, further stirring Lucy's interest. I couldn't believe Norma's enthusiastic response with Perry while he tongued her pussy or the way she gave him head, and I would later reflect that she had said something like, "You always do that so good, lover!"

Always?

Finally, Perry began teasing his dick into Norma, then withdrawing, then repositioning her on the bed and doing this over and over again, never going at it steadily in one position.

This finally sent Lucy over the edge, and she cried, "That's it, Perry. Come on, start fucking her good now! Give her that big cock of yours!"

Perry seemed to know his cue, but he continued to tease a little longer and then rolled Norma onto her back and began fucking her like there was no tomorrow. This was apparently what usually pushed Lucy into readiness.

By now, Nature had taken its course with me and I was aroused too, though not into the frenzy displayed by Lucy. I climbed onto her and gave her what she wanted.

As we finally took a break for a moment, I looked into the other room and Perry and Norma were still going at it. He held her by her ass, upside down with her head and arms on the floor as he stood over her, driving his dick in and out of her pussy.

Norma was most appreciative of this and loudly conveyed her enjoyment to Perry with groans and cries of "Oh, god, don't stop, Perry!"

He replied, "You got it baby, I won't stop now!" as he sawed in and out of her.

Thinking about it now, I believe that Perry must have taken today's equivalent of Viagra, like those porno video actors. Otherwise, a guy his age couldn't have kept going as long as he did. I was quite a bit younger and still pretty hot, so I could easily go for more than one round, if I do say so myself.

Lucy apparently had assessed this trait in me beforehand, because she raved, "Ooh, I knew you'd be good when I saw you, Chris! Give it to me again, I'm just about ready to come!"

This time, Lucy climbed atop me and we went at it again. I lost count of how many orgasms she had, but it was several. But I had to concentrate on what I was doing more than I would have under normal circumstances.

As Lucy finally moved off of me, sated for now, my mind was completely blown and I was stressed out and exhausted both from what I'd done and what I'd seen. Fortunately, the show seemed to be winding down. Lucy was apparently satisfied, and it wasn't long before she again pressed the button by the mirror and it went dark.

I tried to put myself back together, as did she, but not before I got another unexpected and unwanted surprise. As I was zipping up my trousers, Lucy came over to me and tucked a small envelope into my waistband. She smiled, winked, and said, "That was really nice; here's a little 'thank you' from me."

144

I stared at her, dumbfounded, then found my voice and croaked, "Thank you, Lucy."

We made our way back downstairs. Dressed again, Perry and Norma joined us a moment later. They thanked us for "coming to the party" and we were escorted back out to the garage. Little did we know that the evening held yet more surprises.

By the way, if you're wondering what was in that envelope Lucy gave me, it was ten, crisp $100 bills. Now, some guys might just shrug and think, "what the hell, I'm a stud, I earned it!"

Not me; I felt a mixture of dismay, revulsion, and personal embarrassment in taking money for my "command" performance of an act of marital infidelity. It was a case of fun-for-profit that made me feel terrible.

Meanwhile, in the garage, a big Italian guy I knew as Tony was waiting for us. I knew him distantly; he served in the role of *Capo* or some other "higher-up" in the Organization. And I recalled later that he'd been hanging out with Mustache at that summer picnic in Webster. Another guy, *Tommaso*, was driving; he wore a chauffeur's uniform exactly like my own.

We three got into the back of the limo and were soon on the road again. As I sat there trying to get my head back together, Tony questioned Norma about the party. He obviously wanted to hear all of the lewd details.

"How was it? Did Perry give it to you good?" he queried with lusty interest.

Foolish, foolish Norma! I think she was a bit embarrassed (it was about time!) as she realized that a certain cat was out of the bag as far as our relationship went. She had to have known that I was privy to what had gone on and might have seen the whole thing. But she didn't consider that as a possibility where Tony was concerned. So, instead of telling him what he wanted to hear, the dumbshit downplayed the situation and tried to minimize the encounter.

"Oh, no, not really, that guy's a little bit old for the job and he couldn't do much. It was no big deal." She tried to affect a so-what, no-big-deal attitude.

Immediately, I could see rage coming over Tony's face where he sat across from us in the limo. His body tightened and he sat up straight. Suddenly, he pulled out a handgun and pointed it right into

Norma's face. She gasped and drew back involuntarily. He moved closer across the space between the seats.

"You lying bitch! What a goddamned whore! You enjoyed every minute of it and I saw it all. There was more than one mirror in that room, and I was behind one of them. I watched him doing you-- you were on fire! You loved it, anybody could see that! The two of you were great together, just like real-life lovers."

Tony suddenly laid down the gun.

"Get over there on the other seat, Chris."

I'd been sitting side by side on a bench seat with Norma. Quickly I switched seats with Tony as commanded. I could see that my only salvation was to keep my mouth shut and do what he said. He looked ready to kill somebody.

"Take off that damned dress," he ordered Norma, and she hurriedly complied. Why was I surprised to see that the sexy underwear was missing? At any rate, Norma was sitting there completely naked, with her black dress on the floor.

In the meantime, Tony had unzipped his pants, exposing a very large erect penis. "Get your mouth ready for it, bitch," he demanded.

I watched, stunned, as Norma moved over to Tony without hesitation and began sliding her naked tits up and down his waiting erection. He smiled, "Oh, yeah! That's it, those titties feel good, baby."

My wife proceeded to do things I'd never seen her do before (she'd sure as hell had never done them with me!) as she gave Tony the blow job of his life. At last he came and his semen spurted all over her face and chest after she swallowed some of it. Tony had the decency to pull out a clean towel from under the seat compartment and hand it to her so she could clean up a bit.

My poor brain was overdone after being subjected to this unexpected show.

"Hey, boss, what about me?"

It was the limo driver. He was speaking over the intercom connected to the back seat.

"Sure, Tommaso," Tony laughed. "Your turn now. Pull over and park. Chris, you trade places with Tommaso and start driving us home."

What?? Oh, god. Now another guy was going to fuck my wife, right behind my back this time, literally. Naturally, I did as told. It was all very unreal.

I looked around outside and realized we'd traveled quite a distance and were on a main street I recognized. So, I knew where we were and how to get home. I started the engine and began moving.

In the back seat, I could hear sounds of bodies slapping together. A quick peek in the rearview mirror showed Tommaso fucking Norma quite energetically. He was really going at her. He was probably in his early twenties then and had plenty of stamina. Norma made her enjoyment obvious. Tony must have gotten another hard-on just watching them, as he was goading Tommaso, "That's it, Tom, give it to the bitch! She likes it!"

An overwhelming combination of physical and emotional disgust and fatigue sagged through my body and mind as I drove. Fortunately, I knew the route like the back of my hand, and at such a late hour there was little traffic to contend with.

At last Tony directed me to pull in where we'd left our car. Tommaso had zipped up and gotten himself back together. As the limo stopped, I saw Tony giving Norma a handful of bills. "Here, I guess you earned this after all."

The limousine pulled away and as Norma shivered in the cold night air, I lit into her.

"You stupid, stupid bitch! What were you thinking? You can't insult those guys like that and get away with it! You could have gotten us both killed. They don't care about peons like us, Norma. We're lucky to be standing here alive!"

Norma's face showed her own exhaustion. But I couldn't feel sorry for her, not anymore. She'd just fallen off that pedestal I'd put her on and the crash was deafening. But I still had some questions nagging me, and I asked her, "What happened to that fancy underwear you were wearing, the stuff you got from Victoria's Secret?"

"He--he kept it. Perry kept it. That must be part of the thrill or something."

"How much money did Tony give you?"

Mutely, Norma held out the bills. It totaled $1,500.

We both stared at it.

"Wow, nice money," she said slowly, appearing to realize she'd just had sex for profit.

"Yeah, you had fun and you got paid for it," I replied tersely.

I knew that the money Joe had given to Norma for the sexy underwear had paid for more than just that one outfit. Norma had returned from Victoria's Secret with two shopping bags stuffed with several X-rated pieces. I was damned near certain now that she'd already been and would again be paid by the Mob or someone else for sex on many other occasions, and that she was just pretending to be surprised by the cash. Had I known it for certain just then, I'd probably have gotten my gun and shot us both on the spot.

As it was, the evening had been an exhausting one, and I looked forward to getting a shower and possibly a few hours sleep. It was early Sunday morning, and I always dedicated Sundays to playing with our kids. I needed some rest, ASAP.

When I had some time to think, it all started to fall into place with a frightening realization. Everything started adding up and pieces of the puzzle came together to form a terrible picture of the past year's happenings. Indeed, Norma had obviously already been recruited for sex by the Mob; it had all probably been set in motion back at the summer picnic in Webster. That stupid, supposedly drunken overture made by Mustache was actually their way of seeing if Norma would be interested. Joe's behavior with the gun against the guy's head in the office after I complained had apparently been just for show, to make me think it was really a dressing down for Mustache.

I'm almost certain now that Perry and Lucy had been at that picnic, too, but had kept a physical distance from me and Norma so their presence wasn't marked by either of us at the time.

Obviously, Norma had previously been approached by Joe and others, and I'd been too dumb and still blinded by my love for her (remember, she'd been up on that very high pedestal in my mind and heart) to see how I'd been set up and used. They'd played an elaborate game with me where I was carefully kept in the dark so as not to suspect anything. Along the way, I'd not only been a getaway driver and racketeering assistant, I'd made it possible for the Mob to use my wife--MY WIFE!--for fun and profit. She got her share of both along the way, obviously not caring about me or our marriage.

I suddenly flashed on a lot of other past dots that I should have connected. One of them was a fragment of conversation between Mustache and Tony back at the picnic. I'd been chasing a baseball thrown by one of my children, and passed right by the table where those two guys were sitting. Mustache was saying to Tony, "Yeah, I think she'll go for it. She's one hot bitch and she's really hot to trot. Did you check her out? Wow, what great tits! Yep. I already told Joe that we should make the pitch to her tomorrow."

They'd been talking about Norma--duh!! More dots connected and a lot of other random things also finally congealed in my mind. It all fell into place like a revealing dream, only the reality of it was truly a nightmare. In another burst of memory, I recalled how Norma had disappeared for a short time during the picnic and I'd meant to pursue that issue at the time, but it had fallen by the wayside with so much stuff going on.

I'm sure that Mustache was trying to use his influence and move up in his status with the Mob. Having brought Norma to their attention as a sex player was a sort of feather in his cap and I'm sure he was rewarded for his observations just as I was when I accomplished a particular task well. Come to think of it, after that picnic, Mustache tried hard to hide a smirk on his face whenever he saw me. Since I didn't particularly like the guy to begin with, I just blew it off as part of his unpleasant personality.

I was left with a shitload of heartache as I stood there with that damned, crumbled pedestal at my feet. I'd been blind over the years as to how often I'd tripped over the pieces of it as it gradually broke down and finally became a pile of rubble.

When a guy realizes that he's been set up and strung along for a long time, feeling humiliation is natural. So is anger. I felt both then. It was time to start cleaning up the mess and see what recovery was possible.

CHAPTER TWENTY-ONE

Well, so the party to end all parties was finally over. It was the Sunday morning following what I can only refer to as that all-out orgy that starred my wife, the ultimate *Mafia* whore. I'd been an incidental and unwilling player and had also been paid for sex, which I found extremely insulting.

Talk about being in over my head; when you don't have a choice and can't say "no" to the boss, you've lost control. And I had lost it, big time!

Given the undeniable evidence that Norma's sexual proclivities and appetite had created a monster, my job was gonna be a tough one. How can a marriage be retrieved from such a ruinous state? The answer was simple: no rescue was possible. I knew it was over between us, and even as we'd driven home after that party, I said so to Norma as she sat beside me in the car.

"It's too bad, but this is the end of our marriage, Norma. There's no way to pick up the pieces now. I didn't want to believe it of you--that you were such a liar, such a two-faced bitch. You've lied through your teeth about everything all these years, and worse yet, you've put your own sexual gratification and desire to fuck nonstop over the welfare of our children, to say nothing of your relationship with me. And now it's obvious you've been whoring for the Mob for quite a while. How you could do this to me--to *us*--well, I just don't get it."

I knew I was on the verge of completely losing it with Norma and I struggled to keep from going into a complete rage. It was close to 2:00 a.m. and I was just plain beat.

I added, "Things are going to change now, big time."

Norma scoffed. "Oh, stop going on about nothing. I'm sure you had your fun with Lucy in that other room. Who are you to talk about liking to fuck?"

"I've never, ever put my sexual desires ahead of the needs of our three children! But you have, without a second thought. I know you've been fucking anything that walks; I know about you and Mike, and Hank, and Howard Foster. And all you've told me and the kids are a pack of lies. While I've been in over my head with the

Mob, trying to make enough money to give us a good life and make sure our kids didn't go without, you haven't upheld your end at all."

"Bullshit!" was Norma's reply.

"It isn't bullshit and you know it. Tell me truthfully for a change: Why has the school called me multiple times because you weren't there on time to pick up the kids? Why is our youngest son always getting into trouble and making it necessary for us to go get him when he's not where he's supposed to be? And what about Roseanne? She's just a little girl, but you've turned her into your personal servant and glorified babysitter. You've even had her lie for you! That's called neglect and abuse."

Norma looked down and said nothing.

We pulled into our driveway. "It's over, Norma" I repeated. "I'll spend the day with the kids as usual, and then on Monday, I'm going to call a lawyer."

"Suit yourself. I'm sure you'll have a heyday," was the brief answer as Norma opened the car door, got out, and then slammed it shut.

It broke my heart that Sunday afternoon, as I played catch, tag, and other games with the kids. This was a ritual I'd followed for years: Sunday was their day and no matter how tired I was, I always got up and put on a glad face for them. Because I *was* glad I had the kids; they were everything to me, my own flesh and blood, created out of love. Only now, love had fled the picture and I had to figure out how we were all going to go on without Norma in our lives.

I'd said I'd call a lawyer the next day. What I did the next day was, while making my delivery rounds, was to drive over to the Crescent Beach area and see if I could find that house where we'd been. We provided supplies to a couple of businesses there, so my being in the neighborhood was perfectly natural. But I couldn't find anything that was definitive. Tony and the hosts had hustled us in and out of that garage so fast that I couldn't see much. In fact, given the absence of any personal items in the house, such as photographs, I thought, maybe that wasn't even the hosts' home. Maybe it was a porn movie shooting site or something. Oh, well, I had much more important things to deal with and it was time to get moving.

Actually, it took about a week before I contacted a lawyer. I guess I should mention that, when I next saw Joe, he inquired as to how things had gone at the party. I told him that everybody seemed happy and it went well. Joe nodded and said that he'd heard the same thing, and he handed me the usual envelope. I knew there would be several hundred dollars in there for me, in payment for my "work" at the party. It was the second time in 48 hours that I'd been paid for sex and I didn't like it, not one bit. I felt humiliated all over again, but I said nothing about that to Joe. And I now felt so different towards him because he'd been in on the whole thing and was nothing if not two-faced.

"Good job, Chris," he said. "Thank you." He smiled.

I wanted to yell and scream and bust somebody's chops instead of acting like a good, compliant little soldier being paid for his dirty work. But I restrained myself and said nothing. After all, I was going to have to pay a divorce attorney pretty soon. Then we discussed other routine business he wanted me to take care of and I left for the rest of the day.

I did finally call a lawyer we knew and arranged to meet with him in a week or so. Then I stayed busy over the next several days. During that time, I performed my usual duties with my regular employer as well as Joe and the boys. Thank goodness there were no remarkable or stressful activities involved with the latter, so my mind was free to pursue other matters. I knew I needed to leave the Mob, but how was I going to do it? The usual lifespan of a soldier like myself was shorter than most men. Only by the grace and generosity of Joe and Stan had I been sheltered from the unspeakable violence and high-risk behaviors that killed most guys in my position. But, would they just let me go now, after everything, with no strings attached? If they did, would I spend the rest of my life always looking over my shoulder? I just had to try, that much I knew.

Life at home was one big misery after another. With the cats all out of the bag now, Norma made no attempt to hide her marital "straying." On the following Saturday, she left in her car, supposedly going to her weekly appointment at the beauty shop. But I suspected that was not her actual destination.

After waiting a few minutes, I set out to follow her. If there was one thing I knew how to do without being noticed, it was tailing someone.

Up the road ahead of me, I could see her left turn signal flashing; she was turning onto a side road where there were a couple of apartment clusters. They were all duplexes. I pulled off the road and waited a couple of minutes, then drove up and made the same turn. About two blocks down the street, I spotted her parked car. Right beside it was Howard Foster's car. I got out and went up to the door, and through a living room window I saw two older people in recliners, apparently sleeping. Oops, wrong apartment! So, I went up the staircase to the other unit, and pounded on the door.

"Open up, Howard and Norma, I know you're in there!"

No one came to the door; all was quiet. But I knew they were in there. I look back on this now and realize that, if cell phones had been available back then, I could have taken photos of the two cars sitting there side by side and other incriminating evidence. Plus I could have called for some personal "back-up" from the boys.

But there was nothing to be done at the time, and eventually, I drove back home. When Norma finally returned, we had it out.

"So, that's where you two lovebirds spend your time, huh, at Howard's apartment. Since his wife kicked him out, that must be costing him something, paying for two places to live."

I was fishing for information at that point; I didn't know if Foster's wife was even on to him yet.

Norma let the last of the cats out of the bag.

"If you must know, we've been living together there for the past three years. His wife doesn't care. When I'm not here, I'm over there with him, and I'm paying my share, too. You're the dumbshit, always thinking I'm going to be here for you. What a jerk!"

Norma slammed out of the house, leaving me standing there open-mouthed. Why was I always the last one to know?

I finally met with the lawyer, after scraping together enough money for a retainer. Yeah, me, who was usually rolling in cash, thanks to the Mob. Not any more. After Norma stormed out, I'd started looking through the house, particularly the little desk where we kept our personal papers, including monthly bills, etc. More surprises! A stack of past-due notices, including for utilities, house payments, and other obligations stared me in the face. The bitch had only been making minimal payments on everything! We were in arrears to the tune of several thousand dollars. Apparently, she'd been sliding our money into that love nest with Howard Foster for a long time.

The next unpleasant surprise was coming up fast. I'd gone to meet with the lawyer to file divorce papers against Norma. When I sat down in his office, he seemed to have trouble with his mouth; his face was working like he was trying to speak and couldn't quite do it.

In the meantime, I'd opened my wallet and asked him how much he would need for the retainer. I saw his eyes narrow and the puckering around his lips increased. Finally, he said, "Uh, Chris, I'm sorry, there's a problem here. Your wife has already engaged my services and I can't represent you both in a divorce case like this. I can refer you to a colleague."

"WHAT?? Where'd she get the money so fast for your retainer?" I wanted to know. "She's drained off all the household money to pay for her love nest with Howard Foster."

"It's been taken care of," he replied smugly, "She called me before you did and came in to, uh, give me her retainer."

And that's when I knew: Norma had fucked the attorney, too, so he would represent her for her pussy-related services. Was there no shame to the woman, no shred of decency left in her? Apparently not. So, I stormed out of his office, checked around with friends, and found another attorney to represent me.

Norma continued to share the house together and I tried very hard to be home with the kids as much as possible. But I still had to earn us a living and couldn't be there all the time. The next day, I pulled into the driveway after work. I could see by the kids' faces that something had happened.

"Where's your mother?" I asked, already knowing she wasn't there and that they were upset.

"She went to the store," Roseanne told me. Either she was lying or she didn't really know where Norma had gone.

Then my older son piped up. "Dad! Mrs. Foster came over here and threw Mr. Foster's clothes all over the yard and driveway. Why'd she do that?"

I looked around and didn't see anything there. "Where?" I asked.

"Oh, he came over and picked them all up," Roseanne put in. "Mom said it was all a misunderstanding or something."

Right, a misunderstanding. Just another indicator that things were spiraling out of control.

"Come over here," I said gently to my daughter. I walked her over to a quiet corner of the yard to talk to her alone.

"Now, Honey, I want you to tell me what really happened. Did Mrs. Foster say anything while she was here?"

Roseanne looked troubled. "Well . . . yes."

"What did she say?" I tried to smile encouragingly and I put my arm around her.

"She said that Mom could have him--Mr. Foster--if she really wanted him, that she was through with his games and he could go to--to--*you know where*. And she said that they've been shacked up for years and aren't fooling anybody. What does that mean?"

Roseanne's little face was so sad and serious. It broke my heart. I tried to reassure her with a hug.

"Okay, Sweetie, I know what she probably said. Don't worry, it's all right. Now let's go into the house. Aren't you hungry? *I* am!"

I smiled at her, and she grinned back. Whew! What a mess and my children were right in the middle of it.

I started preparing dinner, and the food was almost ready when, about thirty minutes later, Norma walked into the kitchen. The kids were watching TV in the rec room, so we had the kitchen to ourselves for the moment.

"So, just what the hell is going on?" I raised my voice. "Jesus god, you don't care what you do to those kids, do you? If you have to be with Foster, keep your damn fights private. Don't air your dirty laundry--or his clothes--on our doorstep!"

"Oh, for Pete's sake!" Norma sputtered. "It was all a misunderstanding! I got it straightened out."

"Yeah, right. And where have you been since that three-ring circus happened?"

Norma sighed. "Like I said. I took his clothes back to him and called his wife to explain that she totally misunderstood the situation."

"Funny," I responded. "She told the kids that if you want him, you can have him. She's all through with the bastard. She also said that you two have been shacked up for years--not a few days. That's exactly what she said to Roseanne."

"Bullshit!!" Norma yelled, and I yelled over her. I couldn't help myself.

"You're a goddamn cheating bitch and I don't believe anything you say anymore. You don't care about our children or me! All you do is play both ends against the middle, all of the time, lying through your teeth. You've just gotta be spreading your legs--or opening your mouth--all the time for any guy you meet. That was obvious at that party at the lake. What a whore! Some mother you are! Some cheating wife you are, too!"

"Go to hell. Fuck you!" was Norma's reply, and the irony of that rejoinder wasn't lost on me. We shouted a few more things at each other and then she left the room to change her clothes.

I finished the meal preparation by myself and got the kids washed and ready for dinner. It was hard to sit and talk normally with them, but I did my best. Swallowing food, however, was impossible for me.

"Why aren't you eating, Daddy?" my younger son asked.

"Oh, I had coffee and a snack this afternoon with one of my coworkers, and I'm just not hungry. That'll teach me to spoil my dinner with sweets, huh?" I winked at my son. We were always telling him not to eat sweets before dinner. I laughed at my own joke. I'm sure the excuse sounded hollow, but they appeared to have bought it and we turned the conversation to more pleasant things.

"Where's Mommy?"

"Oh, I think she's taking a shower. She's not hungry, either." I lied so glibly to my own flesh and blood. What else could I do?

The next day, at the Market, I went in to Joe's office. "Can I talk to you, Joe? Privately?"

Joe looked up and studied me for a moment. "Sure, Chris. A.J., would you go check on Dad and make sure he's doing okay?"

A.J. could take a hint. He mumbled something like "Sure" and got up and left, closing the office door behind him.

"So, what's going on, Chris?" Joe's face was friendly.

"Well, I hate to say this, but I don't know what else to do, Joe. Things are really falling apart at home. You know that Norma went to that party willingly and now I realize that she's been cheating on me and neglecting our kids for a long time.

"In fact," I looked Joe straight in the eye, "she and another guy, Howard Foster, have actually been shacked up, living together off and on for the past several years. Norma's been taking our household money to help pay the rent for their apartment. His wife got wind of it and came over and threw his clothes all over our yard. So, they're through, too. She's apparently fucking the divorce attorney into the bargain."

I took a deep breath, trying to calm myself. Joe remained silent. I wasn't going to bother telling him that another recent, somewhat mysterious incident involving Norma had suddenly made sense and was further proof of her long-term duplicity. Just before I found out about her long-time affair with Howard Foster, she'd been working part-time at a small jewelry store, and one day I realized she was wearing a new wedding ring, much different than the one I'd given her.

When I asked her where she got it, she claimed that the diamond had fallen out of the original ring and the shop owner offered her a trade on the new one. At the time she said this, I had my suspicions but said nothing. She'd recently quit that job and was doing the paper route. At the first opportunity I got, I went to the jewelry shop and asked the owner about the new ring.

"Did she pick it out herself?"

Mr. Johnson shook his head, "No, she came in with an older gentleman and they selected it together."

That older gentleman was none other than Howard Foster. And the incident had happened several years ago.

It really burned me as I realized that, at the time, our daughter was asking to have her bedroom repainted but Norma had said there wasn't enough money in the budget just then. Of course there wasn't. She had been siphoning money out of the household funds for a long time to pay for the apartment she and Howard were getting together. Boy, was I blind or what! I'd been so busy trying to make a living that I didn't see what was happening right under my nose. *Because I didn't want to.*

I shook myself back to the moment and continued my conversation with Joe.   "I just don't see how I can keep up this pace anymore, Joe. I've gotta do something to protect my three children and I'm always so far from home here in the city. Norma's probably going to move out any day and doesn't give a damn about what happens to them."

I continued, "We're totally broke, since she took all of the household money and our savings to help pay for her 'love nest with Foster. So, it's on me to pick up the ball and run with it. I've gotta get those children into a more stable situation. As much as I've enjoyed my association with you, Stan, and the others--and believe me, I've appreciated everything you've done and your incredible generosity--I need to leave the Organization. Is that possible? I mean, without having to pay or --?"

Joe looked at me and I thought I saw kindness in his eyes. He was, after all, a family man, too. To him, sex was mostly just business. Family was something entirely different.

"Of course, Chris. I understand. Yes, you can go and don't worry about anything hanging over your head. The truth is, you've done an outstanding job for us. Stan and I especially have been very impressed. We always knew we could trust you; you 'made your bones' with us and did it all very well. Your loyalty has been appreciated. You don't owe us a thing. The fact is, you'll leave in good stead and always have friends here; should you ever need to call in a favor, you've got it."

He went on. "You're a good family man and I admire you for putting your children's welfare first. That's what a real man does. And I'm sorry about your wife and how your marriage is ending. You know," Joe said, looking me straight in the eye, "It wouldn't really solve anything as far as that issue goes, but we could still 'take her out' if it would make you feel better."

"No, no!" I exclaimed. "She's still the kids' mother and that means something, at least to them. They've through so much upheaval and disappointment, I don't want to add to the chaos."

Little did I know just then how much worse the chaos would get.

Joe nodded. "I think that's the right attitude, Chris. As I said, you're free to leave the Organization, with no strings attached. I know I speak for Stan when I say that we wish you the very best."

The relief I felt was indescribable. I knew all too well that most people in my position would have just been taken for a little ride out to the countryside and been shot. It took me a moment to compose myself, then I smiled the happiest smile I'd shown in years, realizing that life would go on after all.

"Thanks, Joe. Boy, do I appreciate this. Naturally, I'll stay around and take care of any loose ends before I go. Is there anything--?"

Joe shook his head. "Nope, everything around here's running just fine. Why don't you plan to make Friday your last day?"

I nodded. "That will be just fine. Thanks again, Joe." I grabbed his hand and shook it fervently.

"No problem." Joe smiled. "As I said, we've always known you were a family man and you need to take care of yours just like we take care of ours." He unlocked a desk drawer and pulled out something. "Here. Take this with my blessings; maybe it will help you out a bit. Drop by and say goodbye before you go, okay?"

"Sure will."

I walked back out to the produce company's station wagon in the parking lot with an extra $2,000 cash in my pocket. How ironic. The Mob could take whatever it wanted and push my marriage over the brink with its greedy demands, and then turn around and act like Dracula was really somebody's mother.

A few days later, I came home to find the children very much alone. All three were crying.

"Daddy, Daddy, Mommy went to live with Mr. Foster! She says she doesn't want to be with us anymore. Mommy doesn't love us!" They all sobbed and my younger son wailed. "Why, Daddy, why?"

I was stunned that Norma could do something so low and mean. They were so young and innocent. I tried to comfort the children, but it was hard. Somehow, I had to reassure them that we would all "be okay." They were utterly confused and miserable. Roseanne, the oldest, was nearly 12, and the other two were nine and eleven. They were much too young to cope with this ugliness.

That night, after all three of the kids were tucked into bed and asleep, I sat down with a drink for myself, and I cried, too. I cried for them and their pain, and I cried for having lost the love of my life. After everything I'd been through, the future looked very bleak. All my dreams, my white picket fence fantasy, the ambitions I had for our future and that of the children, were gone, vanished like heaps of sand in the tide. I was just a couple of weeks short of my 32nd birthday, and was going to have to start all over with my life.

That was the saddest night of my life. Then I started getting angry; it was the only self-defense I had against the overwhelming situation. I had to stay strong for the kids; they were going to need me in their corner.

CHAPTER TWENTY-TWO

Norma came back to the house to pick up something she'd forgotten. Fortunately, the kids were at school and not there to witness our confrontation.

"You damned, lying whore! So now you're fucking my attorney, too. I'm going to make sure you never see those kids again!"

"Oh, what makes you think I want them around? I've played babysitter and nursemaid long enough. I deserve to enjoy life without the hassle." She smirked and looked through a closet for something with an unconcerned attitude.

"Get out! Just get out of this house! You're not welcome here anymore."

"Sure, fine, anything you say. But it's my house, too."

Calmly, Norma walked out the door.

Well, I'd started a new job closer to home, nothing to do with produce or the Mob. And, dumb me, I forgot about the need for changing the locks, and soon found that, when I wasn't home, Norma was coming over and helping herself to whatever she wanted.

First, she took our brand-new, top of the line vacuum cleaner, a big loss since I was trying to keep the house especially clean as it went up for sale. Then--and this is what pissed me off the most--she took almost all of our children's photographs and then also helped herself to all of the personally-autographed programs and other mementos from the country singers and other celebrities we'd met through Joe Camp's generosity.

It would take a whole book by itself to describe what happened over the next year, so I won't do it here. But the highlights include the kids being jerked around unmercifully until they didn't know which end was up. For someone who said she didn't care about the kids, Norma suddenly did a turn-around and applied for custody of them. They were living with me, but the bitch somehow got a court order allowing her to send a sheriff's deputy over and haul them out of the house in their pajamas in the middle of the night.

What a caring mother! To subject her own children to such a traumatizing, drama-queen action was just unbelievable. That's when I knew I would never, *could* never forgive the bitch. And I never have.

What's worse was that the very next day, the kids were taken away from her because Howard Foster had slapped my daughter, Roseanne, and she telephoned the police. A judge called me and told me to come to the courthouse and pick up my children.

That was so traumatic for those poor little kids, and I was in a turmoil, trying to figure out how to provide a stable home life for them amidst all of the insanity.

I went through seven--count 'em, seven!--lawyers to finally get the divorce put through. It was a female lawyer who finally went to bat for me. When I got the kids back and safely in my permanent custody, Norma was ordered to pay child support. But she never paid a dime of it--ever.

I never did find out how she got away with that; anybody else would have gone to jail. The court ordered her to be checked out and one of the court staff was able to find out that Norma was manipulating and probably fucking every man involved in order to get her own way. So, she kept receiving favorable reports as to her compliance, and zero follow-up compelling her to pay child support. Norma really didn't want the children, that was obvious, but she used them to hurt me as much as possible. She sure didn't have their welfare at heart.

It was an awful time. Hell, I even socked the bailiff in the court room, I was so wound up and pissed off by her shenanigans. That sure didn't help matters. I became a well-known individual in the local courts and law enforcement system. My temper was stretched to the max and it didn't take much any more for me to go berserk. The only good part about that was that actual ballistics never came into the picture. I'd had to turn in my weapons when I left the Mob, and that kept me from blowing away several people, I'm sure.

One of the other things Norma did between the time she left and the time the divorce was granted really burned me up. She'd stop by the house frequently, when I was at work, and each time she'd tell the kids that I was no good.

One time, I'd bought some groceries ahead for dinner with a female friend who was coming over. When I arrived with the friend, Norma started taking the groceries for herself. When I stopped her, she threw water all over my friend and tried to start a fight.

That was unbelievable. Norma was like the proverbial dog with a bone; he doesn't really want it, but he doesn't want anybody else to have it, either.

Now, I was still trying to be fair and just about this mess. At the time, we had two cars; both were in my name only. Norma needed a car and I figured I'd still try to be nice and sign the papers for one over to her to get new plates on it. So I did.

What was I thinking? Why didn't Howard Foster give her a car? Answer: he and his wife had five or six children, and he wasn't likely to be able to shirk paying child support. So Norma was forced to kick in everything she could--and she did.

When it came to selling our home, we had a buyer and everything was set for the sale. But Norma refused to be reasonable and sign the papers.

Her reason? "I'm not going to make anything easy for you!"

What the hell kind of logic was that? *She had left me and the kids*, not the other way around. I'd remained generous to a fault, offering to split the proceeds from the house sale right down the middle. But she continued to act as though she was the offended party and that I'd been the bad guy all along.

The kids didn't know whom to believe, and I have struggled for the past 40 years to convince them that I was not one hundred percent to blame for our nasty split-up. While all the chaos of the divorce proceedings, difficult home sale, and other issues were going on, I had no home for them to live in. They had to be put in foster care, all in different homes, four several months.

It was not a fun experience for any of them, and they blamed me mostly for it. They were still pretty young, with the oldest being around 13 by the time the divorce was finalized. There was no way for them to work through or resolve anything. They should have gone through counseling to help them, but that never occurred to me. Their mother ignored their existence for the next ten years, and yet somehow, they overlooked that fact and thought it was all my fault.

I will say this: none of them liked Howard Foster, especially my sons. They still don't, and don't even want to hear his name mentioned to this day.

I'm sure that, in the dictionary, under the word "bitch" it says, "see *Norma*." If it doesn't, it certainly should.

Only just now, as I write this book, have my boys started to be more positive towards me on the subject and no longer blame me so much. Both of my sons recently acknowledged that they were aware that Norma left us, not the other way around, and that when she did, it was to live with Howard Foster. However, they still have no idea that their mother was such a whore and I haven't had the heart to tell them. It's possible that one of them may eventually read this book and learn the truth. I'll cross that bridge when I come to it. Neither of them reads much and probably wouldn't even notice if it were on a newstand right in front of them.

My daughter, now 56 years of age, still wants me to get back together with their mother--some 40+ years later. She seems to be caught in a time warp or something and simply won't or can't accept that it isn't going to happen. The result is that she hates my present wife, blames her for everything, and does little to disguise that hatred. I've tried talking to her one-on-one about this many times to no avail. She'll nod and say she understands, and then go right on acting like she hasn't heard a word. While it sounds awful to say, I'd love to be a fly on the wall and watch her reaction to finding out what a worthless, cheating bitch her mother was--if that ever happens.

It's a wonder that I was able to get on with my life and eventually marry someone I could trust who loved me in spite of my background. What's even more marvelous is that she trusts me after everything I've done.

EPILOGUE

In case you're wondering, I did have one more encounter and offer I had to refuse with the Mob. It was a few years later in the early 1980's; I was divorced from Norma and married to another woman, not my present wife. (Yep, it took me three marriages to get it right!) By the way, Norma married Howard Foster and he died a few years ago, but that's also another story unto itself. Life is full of stories isn't it?

One day, we drove to a major shopping mall in Rochester, and I suddenly spotted a tall, familiar figure strolling towards me. It was Stan Valenti. He was flanked by two bodyguards; actually, I'd spotted them first and then saw Stan. There was no mistaking that distinguished face and physique, even from a distance.

As we shook hands and chatted superficially, I suggested to my wife that she go on into a particular store and I'd join her shortly. Stan suggested getting together soon for a more extensive talk, and I told him that we owned a small gift and book store in a nearby town; he could speak with me there.

Sure enough, he walked in a few days later, bodyguards in tow (which freaked out my wife a little). He asked if we could speak privately and I took him down to our basement storeroom.

"Chris, I'll put it to you straight up." Stan spread out $2,000 in hundred-dollar bills on a packing crate.

It turned out that he wanted me to launder money through my store, and emphasized that there would be plenty of benefits to me if I consented. However, I declined, saying that my wife was in fragile mental and physical health and that I just couldn't handle the risk of losing the store if we were caught.

Stan said he understood, but added that if I ever changed my mind, to give him a call. In fact, he came back to my store several more times, hoping that I would reconsider in his favor. He even brought his wife with him on a couple of occasions. The two sat on high stools at our store counter and we all chatted.

At one point, my wife stepped out from behind the counter to go get something, and when she returned, her eyes were as big as saucers. She said nothing, but after the Valentis left, she stammered,

"Chris--he--he had a gun strapped to his ankle. I saw it when I went around the end of the counter, where his pant legs had ridden up."

She was clearly more nervous than her usual high-strung self.

"Yeah, well, don't worry about it, honey," I chuckled. "He's not going to bother us, much less shoot us. Stan's a nice guy."

And he was.

Other similar offers were made to me, too, and I declined them all. I'd had enough of looking over my shoulder constantly and sitting with my back to the wall. I never ratted out Stan or anybody else, but, in due course, the authorities finally connected the dots and were able to put Stan Valenti out of business. His brother Frank had been jailed for his bombing activities and then retired to Arizona. Stan couldn't take the heat and moved outside of Rochester, where he ran a gambling operation and became an important Associate to the Buffalo family. He attempted to return to power in Rochester later on, but did not succeed.

Meanwhile, that playboy, Sammy G, that handsome Rochester Mob kingpin and Georgia Durante's frequent escort, had subsequently met his death in a much-publicized car bombing incident at a restaurant in Rochester on April 28, 1978. There is still speculation as to exactly who engineered his death; it did take two tries before they got him. Sammy knew he was a target, but still tried, by showing himself, to keep his own troops active while the B team members were well hidden. Protected, he thought, by two overstuffed bodyguards, Thomas Torpey and Thomas Taylor, Gingello continued to be prominently seen in public places.

The opposition had a plan to lower a bomb down the chimney of Sammy's house, but that idea was scrapped when they realized his house didn't have a chimney. Well, duh! Another plan involved planting a bomb in a child's toy in front of the house, but that would have posed too big a risk to neighborhood children.

On March 2, 1978, a killer hiding in the trunk of a car in the parking lot of the Blue Gardenia Restaurant triggered a bomb hidden in a snow bank near the entrance to the restaurant. The ensuing explosion sent Sammy airborne, but he wasn't seriously injured.

Undeterred, Gingello continued making his regular social rounds and hitting the hot spots. On April 23, 1978, at 1:15 a.m., Sammy stopped at Ben's Cafe Society on Stillman Street in

Rochester. This was the third club stop for him and his two bodyguards and two young nephews.

At around 2:00 a.m., the nephews left, and a short time later Gingello and his bodyguards walked out. Sammy got into the driver's seat of a black Buick (borrowed) and closed the door. The two bodyguards also got in, but before they could close their doors, a bomb placed under the car was detonated by remote control.

Fortunately for the bodyguards, they were blown right out of the car, with one of them suffering just a broken foot. Sammy didn't fare as well. Gingello's right leg was blown off below the knee and his left leg was nearly severed at the thigh. The powder from the explosion caused his whole body to be blackened. He was rushed to Genesee Hospital; he died at 3:35 a.m. from shock and loss of blood. The city had lost a prominent home-town gangster.

Following that incident, there was a real flurry of violence, investigations, and arrests over the ensuing years. Some were Mob arrests, other were police officials and other public figures whose participation in the corruption and crime activities had finally forced them into a corner.

However, organized crime has been around for a long time. Intense interest in the subject was probably a result of the enactment of Prohibition, since corruption in all of its facets ran rampant at the time. The subject's popularity has never waned. A recent news piece I heard recently stated that organized crime is presently responsible for literally billions of dollars generated in the drug trafficking business. That doesn't surprise me.

The Rochester Mob dwindled down for a while, but I 've heard rumors that they're slowly getting a bit of a toehold there again. However, I also have heard that the Russian Mafia boys have done their best to squeeze the Italians out of a lot of business all over this country. And, I've been told that they are far more ruthless than the Italians. I guess that's possible, but I don't want to know for sure.

Nevertheless, all told, the Italian *Mafia* sure had its heyday in Rochester, and I'm amazed that I have lived to tell about it. But I must admit, even after all these years since, it's still an automatic reflex for me to sit with my back to the wall in restaurants and other public places. A guy can't be too careful.

THE END

#####

ADDENDUM

AMERICAN MAFIA (La Cosa Nostra) STRUCTURE

BOSS--The head of the family, usually reigning as a dictator, sometimes called the don or "godfather." The Boss receives a cut of every operation taken on by every member of the family. Depending on the Family, the Boss may be chosen by a vote from the Caporegimes of the Family. In the event of a tie, the Underboss must vote. In the past, all the member of a Family voted on the Boss, but by the late 1950's, any gathering such as that attracted too much attention.

UNDERBOSS--The Underboss, usually appointed by the Boss, is the second in command of the Family. The Underboss is in charge of all the Capos, who are controlled by the Boss. The Underboss is usually first in line to become Acting Boss if the Boss is imprisoned or dies.

CONSIGLIERE--Consigliere is an advisor to the family. They are often low-profile gangsters that can be trusted. They are used as mediators of disputes or representatives or aids in meetings with other Families. They often keep the Family looking as legitimate as possible, and are, themselves, legitimate--apart from some minor gambling or loan sharking. Often, Consiglieres are lawyers or stock brokers, are trusted and have a close friendship or relationship with the don or Boss. They usually do not have crew of their own, but still wield great power in the Family. They are also often the liaison between the Boss and important "bought" figures, such as politicians or judges.

CAPOREGIME (or Capo)--A Capo (sometimes called a Captain) is in charge of a crew. There are usually four to six crews in each family, possible even seven to nine crews, each one consisting of up to ten Soldiers. Capos run their own small Family, but must follow the limitations and guidelines created by the Boss, as well as pay him his cut of their profits. Capos are nominated by the Underboss, but are typically chosen by the Boss himself.

SOLDIER--Soldiers are members of the Family, and can only be of Italian background. Soldiers start as Associates that have proven themselves. When the books are open, meaning that there is an open spot in the Family, a Capo (or several Capos) may recommend an up-and-coming Associate to be a new member. In the case that there is only one slot and multiple recommendations, the Boss will decide. The new member usually becomes part of the Capo's crew that recommended him.

ASSOCIATE--An Associate is not a member of the Mob, and an Associate's role is more similar to that of an errand boy. They are usually a go-between or sometimes deal in drugs to keep the heat off the actual members. In other cases, an Associate might be a corrupt labor union delegate or businessman. Non-Italians will never go any further than this.

Most recently, there have been two new positions in the Family leadership: the Family Messenger and Street Boss. These positions were created by former Genovese leader Vincent Gigante.

ITALIAN/SICILIAN MAFIA STRUCTURE

CAPOFAMIGLIA - (Don), CONSIGLIERE - (Counselor/Advisor), SOTTO CAPO - (Underboss), CAPODECINA - (Group Boss/Capo), UOMINI D'ONORE - ("Men of Honor").